COSTS, BENEFITS, AND PRODUCTIVITY IN TRAINING SYSTEMS

Greg Kearsley
HumRRO

▲ ADDISON-WESLEY PUBLISHING COMPANY
Reading, Massachusetts / Menlo Park, California
London / Amsterdam / Don Mills, Ontario / Sydney

Library of Congress Cataloging in Publication Data

Kearsley, Greg, 1951–
    Costs, benefits, and productivity in training systems.

    Bibliography: p.
    Includes index.
    1. Employees, Training of—Cost effectiveness.
    I. Title.
HF5549.5.T7K34   658.3'12404   81-22846
ISBN 0-201-10332-X   AACR2

ISBN 0-201-10332-X
ABCDEFGHIJ-AL-898765432

Preface

Personally, I have never found things having to do with financial matters very interesting. The fact that I have no aptitude for dealing with money is easily proven by an examination of my bank account!

So how is it that I have come to write a book on cost/benefits analysis, you ask? The answer is that I have a deep interest in educational innovation. Trying to convince people to try something new almost always requires some kind of justification—often an economic one. In the course of promoting new methodologies and technologies in a wide range of training and educational situations, I have become fairly experienced at conducting cost/benefits analyses. In this book, I have tried to document this knowledge so that it can be useful to others who must also carry out such studies.

Cost benefits analysis is a very important decision-making tool in the business world—essentially the equivalent of statistics in the research community. In fact, the analogy between cost/benefits analysis and statistics is a good one because they should both be viewed as inferential tools intended to *aid decision-making* rather than *provide answers.* Just as a good researcher does not determine the outcome of an experiment solely on the basis of a t test, a good manager does not make a decision on the basis of a single cost/benefits calculation.

Statisticians have been refining their discipline and tools for centuries. Consequently, statistical methods are well developed and based upon a rigorous theoretical foundation. In contrast, cost/benefits analysis is quite recent as a formal methodology. Its application and practice is still very much of an art form (some would say, "black magic"). In this book, I have tried to describe and illustrate a set of models for applying cost/benefits analysis to the training realm.

There are many people who ought to share the praise (or blame) for this work. Terry Compton, Andy Gibbons, and Fred O'Neal are former colleagues who have influenced the ideas found herein.

I am very grateful to Doris Stein for her excellent job of translating my chicken scratches into nicely typed manuscripts, and to Wendy Ebersberger for her editing assistance and the composition of the Index. Finally, I would like to thank HumRRO for financial assistance in completing this book.

Alexandria, Virginia   G. K.
November 1981

Contents

Contents

Contents

Chapter One

Introduction

Who Needs It?

As a manager or administrator in an organization, you are *accountable* for certain projects or activities. Being accountable means that you have to respond to the following types of questions:

- What are you doing now?
- How much does it cost?
- How can we improve our system?
- What will the improvement cost?
- How long will the improvement take?
- What cost savings or benefits will the improvement produce?

Cost/benefits analysis is a methodology or set of procedures that allow you to answer these questions. More specifically, cost/benefits analysis allows you to:

- Justify existing training programs.
- Achieve a better understanding (hence, control) over a training system.

- Determine how to reduce training expenditures and, hence, increase efficiency.
- Determine how to improve training results through increased effectiveness.
- Evaluate the feasibility or payoffs of a proposed training program.

To the extent that you must deal with these kinds of questions, this book will be of interest to you. While the book focuses specifically on cost/benefits analysis of training in the business, industrial, and military domains, it is just as applicable to elementary, secondary, and higher education. Despite the differences in settings, corporate directors, school board members, and university governors tend to be persuaded by the same kind of arguments: those based on facts and figures!

What Is It?

In its simplest terms, managing training and educational programs can be reduced to a kind of balancing act between *costs* and *results* (Figure 1-1). The costs are those incurred in planning, developing, conducting, and evaluating instructional programs. The results are those outcomes that you expect to produce as a direct or indirect consequence of the instruction. These outcomes typically include improved job performance or better employee attitudes, satisfaction, or morale. Your job as a training manager or educational administrator is to keep training costs and results in balance.

So, we have the following definition of cost/benefits analysis:

Cost/benefits analysis: A technique or method for assessing the relationship between results or outcomes and the costs required to produce them.

Under normal circumstances, you want the most results for the least costs. However, as the wise saying goes, "You don't get somethin' for nothin'." Generally, to get better results, your costs must increase.

There are three terms that describe how well you are balancing your costs and results: efficiency, effectiveness, and productivity.

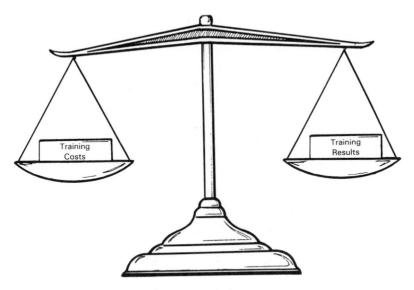

Figure 1-1   Purpose of Cost/Benefits Analysis

Improved efficiency means that we have achieved the same results with fewer costs.

Improved effectiveness means that we have achieved better results with the same costs.

Improved productivity means that we have achieved better results with fewer costs.

As you can see, improved productivity means improving both efficiency and effectiveness at the same time, or put simply:

Improved Productivity = Doing More with Less.

If your goal is to reduce your training expenditures or trim the budget, then improved efficiency is probably of most interest. If the problem is to improve the results of training, then improved effectiveness will be of most interest. If the concern is to do both (cutting training costs and producing better results), then improved productivity is the focus. Since the use of technology often allows us to simultaneously reduce costs and improve outcomes, it is often associated with increased productivity.

You may have heard of "cost effectiveness" and "cost efficiency" studies. In general usage, people do not mean to make a real distinction between effectiveness and efficiency, so both of these terms can be taken as synonymous with "cost/benefit analysis." However, if you want to be technically accurate, a cost effectiveness study would focus on how to improve training outcomes, while a cost efficiency study would focus on how to reduce training expenditures. Even though you now know the difference, it is unlikely that you would want to pick a fight over the distinction!

You might be interested in how cost/benefits analysis relates to other aspects of the training cycle, particularly instructional analysis and evaluation activities (Figure 1–2). It is common to conduct needs, goals,

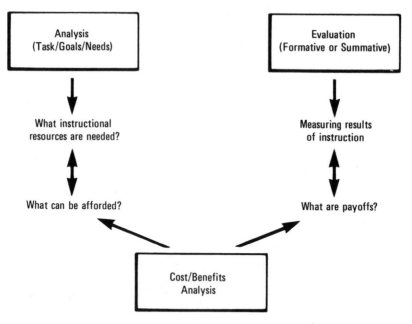

Figure 1-2 Relationship between Major Instructional Development Activities and Cost/Benefits Analysis

and task analyses during the initial design of a training program or system. These analyses ultimately define what instructional resources (e.g., materials, media, personnel) will be involved. Evaluation (either formative or summative) involves the measurement of the effects of an instructional program in terms of increased student achievement, improved job performance, etc. Cost/benefits analysis asks the questions: "What can be afforded?" and "What are the (actual or expected) payoffs?" Thus, cost/benefits analysis is associated with both these phases of the training cycle.

How Do I Do It?

Conducting a cost/benefits analysis involves five major steps, which will be considered in detail in subsequent chapters.

1. Formulate the Question/Problem

Cost/benefits analysis normally begins with some question or problem that you may have raised yourself or that is brought to your attention by an individual (i.e., your boss). Typical questions are:

- How can we increase the annual training throughput to meet some anticipated future demand without greatly increasing the training expenditures?
- How can we improve a certain dimension of job performance (e.g., safety, production, sales, morale, etc.)?
- Should we begin using a new technique/technology in our training program?
- What would be the effects of reducing the training budget or eliminating certain training programs?
- How much would it cost to provide training for a new product/machine and what is the best way to do it?
- What's wrong with our current training system or a particular training program?

Usually, the questions will not be in quite as general form as those listed. Instead, they will be phrased in terms of the specific details of your organization or training setting. The first step in conducting a cost/benefits analysis is to formulate the question or problem in as general terms as possible so that you can see what dimensions or variables are really important.

2. *Develop a Model and Assumptions*

A model is simply a way of representing relationships between concepts. In the context of cost/benefit analysis, the concepts of interest are those associated with the various costs and the results of your training system. The relationships are those connecting the costs and results. You need a model (i.e., representation) because you are probably going to have to explain those relationships to others and because you want things to come out the same each time you compare them.

As you know, models come in a variety of forms. There are physical models (e.g., of cars and airplanes), mathematical models, and analogical models (like metaphors, for instance). Models may be informal "rules of thumb" (for example, the sun rises in the east and sets in the west) or formal equations. Models may be manual (i.e., worked out by hand) or automated (i.e., require computers).

In conducting cost/benefits analyses we will be primarily concerned with formal models that are described either graphically or mathematically. All of the models discussed in this book are in manual form, although they could easily be automated (and, in fact, have been).

When a model is constructed, it necessitates making assumptions. In fact, saying that a relationship exists between any two concepts (in our case, costs and results) is an assumption. The way to change an assumption into a fact is to collect some data that support the relationship. Oftentimes, an assumption is fairly obvious and is accepted as a fact without data. On the other hand, some assumptions will be hotly disputed and need to be backed up by data.

When you have formulated a question or problem, your next step is to try to identify what the relevant cost and outcome variables are and how they relate to each other. In doing this, you are constructing a model and making assumptions. To use your model and check your assumptions, you will need to collect data. This is the next step.

3. Collect Data

There is really no way to do a cost/benefits analysis without data. The data required may be numerical information (e.g., How many students per year? What is an instructor's annual salary?), or it may deal with locations (Where?), times (When?), or people (Who?). Frequently you will need information on the reasons (Why?) things are done or the way (How?) they are done. In short, your requests may involve:

- Who?
- When?
- Where?
- Why?
- How?
- How much?
- How long?

The data you will need can be collected in a number of different ways from a number of different sources:

- *Questionnaires.* Often the information you need can be obtained by asking people to respond to a questionnaire.
- *Interviews.* Talking to somebody (either in person or via phone) is another common way to get information.
- *Observation.* Sometimes the only way to get the information needed is to see what people do in a certain task or situation.
- *Financial documents/reports.* Cost information can often be obtained from documents such as annual reports, budgets, five-year plans, etc.
- *Government.* Many agencies of the federal government, such as the Department of Labor, the Department of Commerce, and the Department of Education, can provide or publish reports and books containing statistical information that can be very useful in cost/benefits analysis.

- *Literature.* Systematic search of periodicals or books may turn up information needed in a study.

Although you will mostly need data after you have formulated the problem and model, it is quite likely that you will need data in order to actually formulate the problem and model. In fact, it is best to think of data collection as a continual and ongoing activity during a cost/benefits analysis.

4. Compute the Costs and Benefits

Having collected your data, you are now in a position to determine what things cost, compare alternatives, and address the question or problem that provoked the study. You will likely be trying to show a cost reduction, cost avoidance, or value-added benefit in your results.

Cost reduction means that you show a way of reducing current expenditures.

Cost avoidance means that you show a way of avoiding certain future costs (e.g., building a new training facility, hiring more instructors, etc.).

Value-added benefit means that you show how to get more out of the current system (e.g., doing something faster, reducing attrition/turnover, etc.)

Another concept likely to show up here is the Return on Investment (ROI). ROI is the ratio of what something returns to what it costs. Thus, if a sales training program cost \$100,000 but increased sales by \$1 million, its ROI would be \$1,000,000 ÷ 100,000 = 10 times. Similarly, if a safety training program costs \$25,000 and it resulted in \$100,000 less in accident payments, its ROI would be \$100,000 ÷ \$25,000 = 4. Obviously, any ROI greater than 1 is worth looking at.

5. Use Your Results

As self-evident as this step seems, it is explicitly included because many good cost/benefits studies fail in this final step. Apart from their use to simply understand a training system, cost/benefits analyses are normally undertaken to *justify* something or *persuade* someone to support a program. Thus, a critical part of the cost/benefit analysis is the presentation of the study. This usually includes:

Background (statement of the problem/question)
Model and assumptions
Methodology (what data was collected and how)
Results (what was found)
Conclusions (interpretation of the results)
Recommendations (what should be done)

Your study may be documented in written form and/or presented verbally. Any of the six parts above could lead to disagreement and rejection of your study. Your statement of the problem may be seen as incorrect. Your model and its assumptions may be considered invalid. Your data may be challenged as inaccurate or out of date. Someone may feel that your findings do not follow from the data, or that your interpretation of the findings (i.e., the conclusions you draw) are not appropriate. Finally, someone may accept your conclusions but think that other recommendations are called for. Remember, on the basis of your study, a significant business decision may be made. Everyone wants to be sure that the decision is correct. Furthermore, it is quite likely that if your study recommends a cost reduction, or new training approach or program, a number of people will have to change the way they do things. People seldom accept changes gracefully!

While you may be thinking of cost/benefits analysis as a one-shot effort to address a specific question or problem (which it sometimes is), you should really think of it as a tool that you are likely to use on a regular and recurring basis. The models developed and data collected in a cost/benefits analysis are precisely what is needed to do accurate planning and forecasting in a training system.

How Will This Book Help Me?

The rest of this book deals with the ideas introduced in this chapter. It will teach you what you need to know to plan, conduct, and evaluate a cost/benefits analysis in a training system. In the next five chapters, you will be introduced to a number of different types of cost models and examples of how these models are applied. After the chapters on models, you will find one on data collection and one on using the results for planning and forecasting activities. The next chapter is a case study that shows how the cost models "fit together." Following the case study is a chapter that discusses *ad hoc* models and other approaches to cost/benefits analysis. The penultimate chapter deals with the cost/benefits of computer-based instruction. The final chapter sums up what you have learned and discusses how to overcome roadblocks and obstacles you can expect to encounter.

One word of caution. This is a practical book, not a theoretical work. It is not particularly formal and certainly not very rigorous. If you find yourself arguing with an economist over anything you learn here, it is probably better to give him or her the benefit of the doubt! On the other hand, what you learn from this book should help you make sound decisions about improving training system efficiency, effectiveness, and productivity.

Chapter Two
Different Models for Different Problems

In the first chapter, the role of models in cost/benefits analysis was introduced. As you recall, a model serves to identify the relationships between costs and benefits, and, in doing so, also requires you to state your assumptions. In essence, the model underlying a cost/benefits analysis represents the way you have formulated the question or problem to be addressed.

In this chapter, four different types of models are described. Each of these models is best suited for addressing certain kinds of problems or questions. After reading this chapter, you should be able to determine which model is appropriate for your needs. Subsequent chapters in the book describe the nature and use of each of the four models in detail.

Resource Requirements Models

The resource requirements model provides a simple and straightforward framework for analyzing the training costs associated with different approaches or delivery methods. It allows the systematic identification of costs associated with each aspect of the training process according to four major categories of resources: personnel, equipment, facilities, and materials.

Figure 2–1 depicts the basic structure of the model. The rows represent five major stages of the training cycle; the columns represent the four major resource categories. Each cell of the matrix can represent a different aspect of training costs. For example, in the development stage of training, there are costs associated with personnel (e.g., artists, writers), equipment (e.g., copiers, cameras), facilities (e.g., offices, studios), and materials (e.g., film, supplies).

By filling in the cells applicable to a certain training setting, the total costs applicable are determined by adding up all of the rows and col-

	Personnel	Equipment	Facilities	Materials
Analysis				
Design				
Development				
Implementation				
Evaluation				

Figure 2-1 Training Resource Requirements Model

umns. In order to compare two training approaches or techniques, the total costs of each are summed across all aspects and resource categories and then compared. Using the model in this way, it is possible to decide if a new training approach or technique could produce cost savings over an existing method.

Note, however, that this method only involves training costs and can only be used to make comparisons about efficiency—not effectiveness. When this model is used to compare two approaches, the assumption is made that the two approaches result in equal training results, i.e., they are equally effective.

The other assumptions made in using this model have to do with the particular aspects of the training system included. Depending on what components of the training cycle are included or excluded, a certain approach may be favored in a cost comparison.

Life Cycle Models

The resource requirements model just discussed provides a way of comparing the costs of two or more different training approaches at a given time. However, it is often the case that cost savings can only be validly determined by taking into account the entire life cycle of the training system.

Figure 2–2 depicts some of the major stages of a training system life cycle relative to costs. Between points A and B, a new training approach is being investigated or pilot tested (the R&D phase). At point B, a decision is made to fully implement the new approach. The slope from B to C represents the start-up costs associated with the new training approach. Costs tend to rise quite steeply during this period as the necessary resources are acquired (e.g., new personnel, equipment, facilities) or materials are developed. Once the new approach is fully implemented (the operational stage), costs tend to remain relatively constant with a gradual increase or decrease. Some interval D–E (typically a year) during this operational phase is taken to provide the "steady state" costs of the system.

At some point in the operational period (point F in the diagram), another approach will be implemented which replaces the existing ap-

13

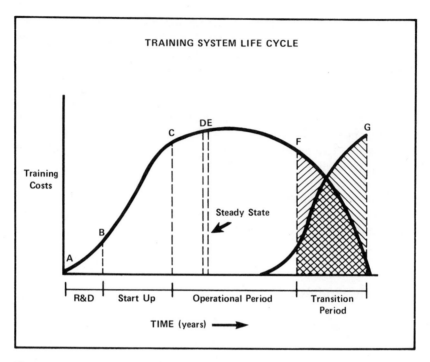

Figure 2-2 Training System Life Cycle

proach. During the transition period (F to G), both the old and new approaches will be in use. The transition costs will include resources for both the old and new approaches.

This model suggests there are four major phases during the life cycle of a training system with different cost dynamics associated with each. During the R&D phase, a relatively small amount of money is spent on feasibility studies, needs analyses, materials or equipment prototypes, try-outs, etc. In the start-up phase, the role and amount of spending increases dramatically as programs are implemented. Once the program is fully implemented, the operational costs level off and often decline. During the transition phase, there are typically two sets of costs to be borne: those of the old program that is being terminated and those of the new (replacement) program that is being started up.

14

In some costing approaches, the R&D and start-up costs are lumped together as "sunk" or "capital" costs and separated from the operational costs since they only occur once, while the latter are ongoing. On the other hand, many costing approaches amortize the R&D and start-up costs across the expected lifetime of the training program. Which approach is most appropriate will depend on the nature of the start-up resources involved (e.g., buildings, equipment, people, etc.) and the financial practices of the organization.

The value of the life cycle model is that it allows you to evaluate the costs associated with each of the four phases to determine if a training program or approach will result in a net cost savings. Thus, a resource requirements model done for the steady state phase of a new program may show considerable savings over an existing one. However, when the start-up phase is considered (e.g., new facilities, equipment, or people required), it may turn out that these start-up costs far outweigh the cost savings that would have been produced during the operational phase.

Benefits Models

Neither the resource requirements nor life cycle model deals with training benefits. They can be used to determine cost savings or cost efficiency, given the assumption that the different approaches or programs compared are equal in their effectiveness. In many instances, this assumption is reasonable. However, in those cases where the explicit purpose of a new training approach is to improve the effectiveness of the training, then it becomes necessary to model expected benefits. For example, it is common to try out a new training technology because it makes something possible that could not be done before. Even though the new approach may cost more, it may be justified in terms of the increased employee proficiency it results in. This is where a benefits analysis is needed.

The basic model underlying a benefits analysis is depicted in Figure 2–3. A benefits analysis must causally link the attributes of a training program with the major goals of the program and ultimately with those of the organization. Figure 2–3 shows that a number of training system

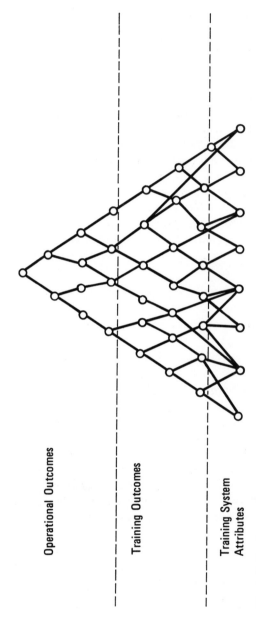

Operational Outcomes

Training Outcomes

Training System Attributes

Figure 2-3 Causal Model Underlying Benefits Analysis

attributes (e.g., media capabilities, testing capabilities, student capacity, etc.) result in certain training outcomes, such as student completion time, retention, attitude changes, motivation, and so on. Training outcomes in turn lead to operational outcomes (e.g., production time, equipment failure rates, sales volume, customer interactions, etc.). When these outcomes are positive, they are benefits (e.g., faster production times, reduced equipment failures, increased sales, reduced customer complaints).

For each training system, a unique set of relationships will exist between training system attributes and training/operational outcomes. Clearly the benefits model for a sales organization will be quite different from that of a manufacturing company or a military unit. To use this model, it is necessary to identify all of these relationships (essentially causal relations) for the training system concerned.

Once the outcomes and their relationships have been identified, the model can be used to identify the relative importance of each training system attribute in term of its payoff on training or operational outcomes. For example, if the amount of "hands on" practice for service personnel is doubled, what outcomes (benefits) will that result in? Will it, for instance, mean that technicians wil be twice as good at maintaining equipment and hence that downtime will be reduced by one half? Or, if the duration of sales training is increased by 50 percent will sales ultimately increase by 50 percent? These are the kinds of questions that benefits analysis addresses.

Productivity Models

We have looked at two models for assessing cost efficiency and one for cost effectiveness. Productivity models are intended to measure both efficiency and effectiveness. To improve productivity, costs or resources utilized must be reduced at the same time training results are increased.

In the educational domain, the measure of training results is usually student achievement (i.e., grades) or number of students graduated. In the training realm, the measure is typically job proficiency skills (e.g., improved sales, customers served, machines serviced, etc.). Improving student achievement scores or job skills by means of better instructional procedures, more skilled instructors, or instructional technology (which reduces resource requirements) increases productivity. The result of associating a specific set of training or learning variables resources with certain performance variables results in a productivity function linking training costs and outcomes.

Figure 2–4 illustrates the basic nature of productivity functions. The straight line (labeled A) on the graph represents an equal increment in improved training outcomes for every increment in increased training costs. In other words, if twice the money is spent on training, the employees are able to do their job twice as well. Curve B represents a training approach in which each improvement in training results is obtained at a considerable increase in training costs. Curve C shows the case where each gain in training effectiveness is obtained for a much smaller

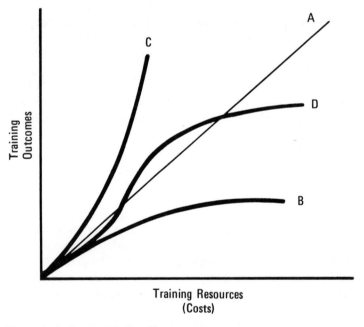

Figure 2-4 Productivity Functions

increase in costs. Finally, curve D is the situation where gains in training effectiveness are initially greater than costs (like curve C) but then become less (like curve B).

While all of these productivity functions are possible, curve D is the most realistic. In the beginning of a program, it is common to get significant improvements for a relatively small effort. However, as we attempt to achieve greater improvement, it comes to take more and more resources. At some point, only negligible improvement is obtained despite considerable resource investments. This is the well known phenomenon of "diminishing returns," which applies in the training world just as much as anywhere else.

The question we are particularly interested in answering is: Which training approach has the most satisfactory productivity function for the level of job proficiency we desire? We want to measure the value of a certain training course, media, technique, procedure, etc., in terms of simultaneously reducing training costs and improving training outcomes. We are especially interested in knowing when a training approach is likely to start showing diminishing returns and hence needs to be replaced. In other words, productivity analysis tells us when we need to switch from one training approach to another (e.g., from lecture mode to mediated self-study or computer-based instruction). To use a transportation analogy, it is a way of knowing when you should walk, when you need to drive, and when you need to use an airplane. As the analogy correctly suggests, productivity analyses are typically complex and situation-dependent assessments.

Which One to Use?

In this chapter four major types of cost/benefits models have been introduced. Each of these models applies to different aspects of cost/benefits analysis, as shown in Figure 2–5. If your primary interest lies in identifying a cost savings (i.e., improved cost efficiency), then either the resource requirements or life cycle models will be appropriate. If you are concerned with assessing costs at a single point in time, then the resource

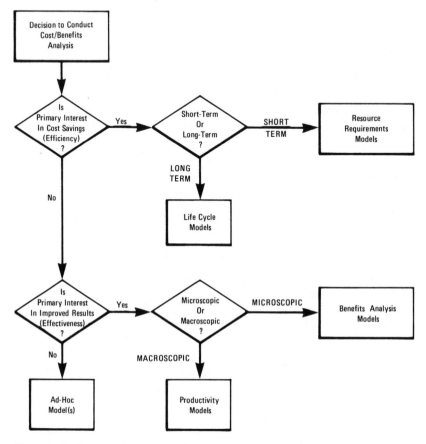

Figure 2-5 Decision Diagram for Selection of Appropriate Cost/Benefits Model

requirements model is sufficient; if you want to assess costs across the entire life cycle, then a life cycle model is needed.

If you need to look at improved results rather than (or in addition to) cost savings, then benefits or productivity models are called for. Benefits models will allow you to determine the relative effects of different training parameters in terms of desired goals and outcomes. Productivity models permit the examination of different cost/benefit functions for a particular training situation. In essence, benefits models let you isolate the relative importance of individual training parameters while productivity models help you assess the summative (and sometimes, synergistic) effect of a set of parameters.

As Figure 2–5 shows, none of these four models may be quite right for you and you may develop an *ad hoc* model. An *ad hoc* model is a unique conceptual framework developed to represent a particular problem or set of relationships. Often, *ad hoc* models will combine or involve subsets of the four major models. Other times, they bear little resemblance to these models and are based on mathematical or statistical models beyond the scope of this book.

The selection of which model to use will basically depend on two factors: What question are you trying to answer? How much money and time can you afford to spend on the cost/benefits analysis?

Clearly, if the question has to do exclusively with costs such as:

• What proportion of our training budget is spent on _____?
• How could we reduce our training costs?
• How much would this approach save us over our existing approach?

then the resource requirements or life cycle models would be appropriate. To differentiate between these two models, simply ask: "Immediately or eventually?"

If the question has to do with training outcomes such as:

• How can we improve our training system?
• What are the benefits of this approach over our existing approach?
• Why does that change result in those specific outcomes?

then the benefits or productivity models are appropriate. The benefits model is needed if there is no detailed understanding of what affects what in the training system. The productivity model is most suited to examining the total effects of different approaches. While both models can often address the same question, one takes a *micro* perspective while the other is a *macro* view.

If none of these four models seem to address the question or problem you are faced with, then you need to develop an *ad hoc* model. You may find that you can construct your *ad hoc* model from studying the four types of models described here, or you may need to consult other books on the subject. (See the last chapter.)

Cost and time are important factors in determining which model to use. Resource requirements models are quite simple and require data that are usually easy to obtain. Consequently, they do not cost very much or take a great deal of time. Life cycle models are more complex and require considerably more data. Obviously, this means that they will cost more and take longer. Both productivity and benefits models require the most data and take the longest to formulate. The more powerful the model, the more time and data required.

This discussion in this chapter should give you a good idea of what model is best suited to your needs. You can now turn to the appropriate chapter and study that model in detail. If you are not sure which model is appropriate, it is a good idea to start with the simplest (i.e., resource requirements) and use the other models on the basis of your experiences with this model. One thing to keep in mind is that the data requirements of the benefits and productivity models are much more sophisticated than the life cycle and resource requirements models. It may be that you are not able to get such sophisticated data from your organization until you instigate the appropriate data collection procedures. Thus, you may have no choice but to start with the resource requirements model since this is the only data immediately available.

The perils and pitfalls of data collection are discussed in Chapter Seven. You should read this chapter thoroughly before attempting to actually conduct a cost/benefits analysis. It will probably save you a lot of time and grief.

Chapter Three

The Resource Requirements Model

Looked at in its most basic terms, cost/benefits analysis has to do with determining what resources will produce what results. Resource requirements models summarize the total resources associated with a particular training approach. By comparing the total resources required for one approach with those required for another approach, potential cost savings can be determined. Remember that the assumption is made in this model that both approaches are equally effective in terms of their training outcomes.

Resource Components

Figure 3–1 lists some examples of resource components in terms of the four major categories: personnel, equipment, facilities, and materials.

Personnel costs include the salaries of students, training analysts, instructional designer/developers, instructors, programmers, managers/administrators, artists, and production personnel. They also include fees for consultants who help design or evaluate the training system/

Equipment	Facilities
Training Devices	Classrooms
• Computer	Laboratories
• Video	Offices
• Trainers	Libraries/Learning Centers
Telecommunications	Carrels
Laboratory Equipment	
Personnel	**Materials**
Instructors	Workbooks
Managers/Administrators	Texts
Clerks	Slides, Tapes
Programmers	Programs
Analysts/Designers	Tests
Evaluators	Paper
Consultants	Film
Artists	

Figure 3-1 Examples of Resource Components

program, and contractors who develop or provide training materials. Expenses associated with personnel (such as travel, temporary accommodations, etc.) are also included as personnel costs. Personnel costs are usually expressed in terms of hourly rates or annual salaries.

Equipment costs cover any equipment required for any aspect of training. This includes devices such as slide projectors, videotape players, or computer terminals. It also includes any equipment used for "hands on" training for operators, service technicians, etc. In addition, any equipment required especially for the production of training materials (e.g., printing presses, cameras) should be included. Equipment costs should include operation and maintenance, as well as purchase costs. Since the total purchase cost of equipment is usually amortized over its anticipated lifetime, it is often considered a "sunk cost" for a resource requirements model and therefore omitted.

Facilities costs are those associated with the operation of training facilities, including all fixtures, maintenance, and upkeep. This would include classrooms, schools, learning centers, offices, production shops, and so on. Often, these costs are provided on a cost-per-square-foot basis.

Materials costs are those required for the design, development, reproduction, distribution, or revision of training materials such as textbooks, slides, tapes, or computer programs. These costs exclude the personnel and equipment costs that are identified separately under the appropriate categories. These figures are usually provided on a per-unit basis (i.e., per book or per tape set).

Training Stages

In order to provide a systematic basis for identifying and comparing the various resources associated with a particular training approach, we need to examine each major stage of the training process. Figure 3–2 depicts the five major stages: analysis, design, development, implementation, and evaluation.

In the analysis stage, the need for a training program is identified (needs assessment) and the major goals are delineated (goals analysis). Also in this stage, the major tasks involved in the job to be trained are described (job or task analysis).

In the design stage, the goals and job/task analysis information is fashioned into instructional objectives that specify exactly what the student is expected to accomplish as a result of each training activity. The objectives also provide the basis for the selection of media. An objectives hierarchy is developed, which indicates the sequence of instruction on the basis of prerequisite skills and knowledge. A curriculum or course design document is developed, which specifies the exact form of each lesson including the content, the practice exercises, tests, and the media.

25

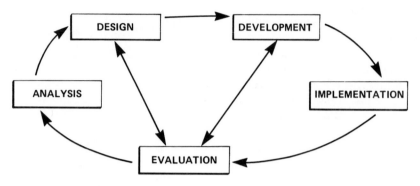

Figure 3-2 Major Stages of the Training Cycle

In the development stage, the materials required for a training program are developed according to the design document. This could include student workbooks, instructor guides, slides or tapes, tests, computer programs, and so on.

In the implementation stage, the training program is given either in classroom format or some form of self-study.

In the evaluation stage, the effectiveness of the training materials and program are assessed. Evaluation usually comes in two forms: formative and summative. Formative evaluation involves the collection of data for the purpose of revising and improving the training materials program, usually beginning with tryouts in the design/development stage. Summative evaluation involves the collection of data to determine if the program is achieving the goals it was originally intended to satisfy.

Obviously, not all training systems will encompass all of the stages as just described. In fact, only a very large training system, such as one would find in a major corporation or the military, is likely to explicitly include all five stages. However, these five stages do usually occur even in the smallest training system, although they are not explicitly identified as such.

An Example: Customer Relations Training

A manager of a retail store observes that clerks are not dealing with customers very well, resulting in complaints. The manager purchases a videotape on customer relations and requires each clerk to watch the tape and complete the accompanying workbook. After the training, the manager observes that clerks interact with customers much better and that complaints have essentially disappeared.

In this simple example, the analysis amounts to the manager's observations along with the data on customer complaints. The design phase amounts to identifying and selecting the customer relations program that meets the training needs. Since the training materials (i.e., the videotape and workbook) already existed, there is no development stage. The implementation of the training program amounted to ensuring that each clerk watched the tape and completed the workbook. The evaluation phase consisted of the manager's observations again and the customer complaint data.

Thus, even in this simple case involving off-the-shelf materials, four of the stages were present. However, if the manager were asked to cost the training resources, it is likely that she would list only the purchase price of the customer relations program. To be complete, the manager should include the cost of her time (and anyone else involved) in identifying the problem (analysis stage), the time involved in selecting and obtaining the training materials (design stage), the operating costs of the equipment (videotape player) and facilities used for the training, the value of the students' time while taking the program, and the time to check the student workbooks (all implementation stage), and finally, the manager's time in determining that the program had worked (evaluation stage).

Incidentally, in case you are wondering why things are not always as simple as this example and under what circumstances you would need to go through all of these detailed steps described, consider a slight twist to the example. This time, the situation is a large insurance company with thousands of clerks using a computer system. The problem is the same: a high number of customer complaints. While the cause of the problem could be poor customer relation skills, it could also be a lack of understanding of the correct inquiry procedures, or a lack of skill in using the computer system. The manager could gamble that the problem is customer relation skills, but it could be a very expensive gamble if she is wrong. Instead, the manager authorizes a job analysis to determine the cause of the problem. The job analysis reveals that some clerks lack customer relations skills, some do not understand the procedures, and some do not know how to use the computer system.

In other words, the problems come from all three causes and training is needed for each. So now training programs must be designed and developed to train clerks in correct customer inquiry procedures and operation of the computer system, as well as customer relations training (which can be bought off-the-shelf). Note, also, that not all clerks need all of the training, so some testing will be involved for proper training assignments.

The Resource Requirements Matrix

Using the resource requirements model simply involves identifying the resources associated with each stage of the training cycle applicable to a particular training situation. This amounts to filling out all of the cells in the matrix shown in Figure 3–3 for each approach you want to compare. Once all of the cells that apply have been filled out, the sum of the cells across all rows and columns provides the total cost of that approach. Put in the form of an equation:

Total	Total	Total	Total	Total
Training =	Personnel +	Equipment +	Facilities +	Materials
Costs	Costs	Costs	Costs	Costs

Clearly, the costs must all be for the same period, usually a year.

In addition to identifying the total cost of a particular approach, the row and column totals of the matrix provide some useful information about the proportion of the resources being expended for a particular type of resource or training activity. For example, it is common for personnel costs to be the most costly training resource (reflecting the labor-

	Personnel	Equipment	Facilities	Materials
Analysis				
Design				
Development				
Implementation				
Evaluation				

Figure 3-3 Resource Requirements Matrix

intensive nature of most training systems), and the implementation stage of the training cycle to be the activity in which most resources are used (reflecting the lack of adequate analysis, design, and evaluation in most training systems). However, different training approaches result in different configurations of training costs across resource categories and training cycle stages. Thus, the matrix not only provides a systematic means for arriving at the bottom line, but it also makes clear the *pattern* of training costs and how this pattern will change with different training approaches.

This point can be seen most clearly if we compare the pattern of costs associated with a traditional classroom lecture course versus the same training program in a self-study format utilizing videotapes and work-books. The major costs in the case of the classroom approach are for instructor salaries and facilities costs in the implementation stage. In the self-study approach, the major costs are for the personnel required to design and develop the videotapes and workbooks, along with the equipment, facilities, and materials needed to develop and deliver the training. Even though more cost categories are involved in the self-study approach, the total cost will not necessarily be more than the classroom approach. The important thing to realize is that the pattern of costs can be quite different between two training approaches. In planning for one approach or the other, different resources would be needed (i.e., different kinds of personnel, equipment facilities, and materials).

An Example: Centralized versus Distributed Product Training

To illustrate how such resource shifts would occur, consider the example of a consumer electronics company that is constantly faced with the need to train its retail store employees on new products. The present approach involves giving the assignment to a staff training specialist who spends four months developing a course on the product and then two months teaching the course to the managers of all the retail stores. The course is one week long and the managers are all flown to a central training facility. After the course is over, the trainer must take the lecture and student notes and turn them into a training manual for managers to use to train their staff. The instructor has responsibility for making revisions to the manual for the lifetime of the product.

While this approach works fine, the travel component associated with the centralized training has become extremely expensive. The company's Vice President of Human Resource Development asks you, as a training analyst, to look into the possibility of decentralizing product training and, hence, reducing the travel costs. After studying approaches being used by other companies, you determine that decentralized product training approaches utilizing videotapes and self-study workbooks appear to be as effective as classroom approaches. Furthermore, it seems that it will save the company $34,000 per product. Therefore, you recommend the decentralized approach to the Vice President.

The costs are as follows for the central classroom approach:

Personnel:	Trainer's salary (6 months)	= $ 18,000
	Travel (200 managers × $1,000/trip) =	200,000
Facilities:	Classroom (1 month)	= 1,000
Materials:	Overheads/handouts	= 400
	Total	$219,400

Figure 3–4 shows how these costs fill out the resource requirements matrix. Note that the trainer is responsible for the analysis, design, development, and evaluation in this approach. There are no major equipment costs involved in the classroom approach.

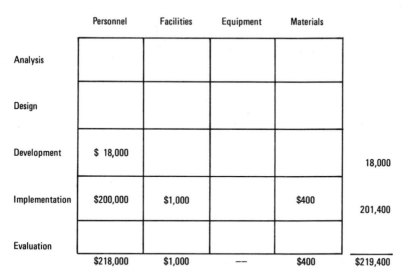

Figure 3-4 Costs for Centralized Approach

Here are the costs for the decentralized approach:

Personnel:	Analysis & design (consultants)	=	$ 20,000
	Videotapes & workbook		
	development/production	=	150,000
	Trainer's salary (3 months)	=	9,000
Equipment:	200 videotape players	=	(100,000)
Materials:	Tape/workbooks duplication &		
	distribution	=	6,000
		Total	($185,000)

Figure 3–5 shows the resource requirements matrix completed for these costs. The analysis and design is conducted by consultants. The videotape and workbook are developed in-house. The trainer is still in-

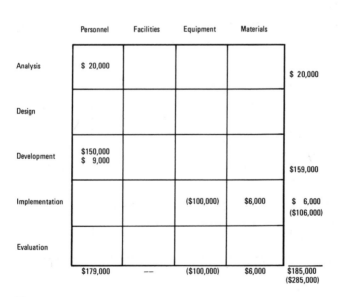

Figure 3-5 Costs for Decentralized Approach

32

volved in terms of providing subject-matter expertise, managing the project, and revising the workbook. The materials costs involve the duplication and distribution of 200 sets of tapes and workbooks. To play the videotapes, a videotape player is needed at each store. However, since the company makes videotape players, it can use one of its own products (which can later be used for a demonstration model or rented) and there is no equipment cost. There are no major facilities costs in the decentralized approach.

Comparing the total costs of the centralized versus the decentralized program, there is a savings of $34,000 ($219,000 − $185,000 = $34,000) in favor of the decentralized approach. In addition, the product training has been standardized for all employees, can be given to all stores at the same time, and has released half of the time of the trainer to work on other projects.

Note that if the equipment had not been available, the decentralized approach would have cost $66,000 more than the centralized approach and would not have resulted in a cost savings. (However, it might have been worth that much if the value added benefits were costed).

Comparing Figures 3–4 and 3–5, it is possible to see how the two approaches differ in terms of resource requirements. Most of the costs in the centralized approach are for personnel costs (specifically, student travel expenses) during implementation. On the other hand, the major costs in the decentralized approach are personnel costs during analysis, design, and development. Furthermore, if equipment costs had been counted, they would have represented the major implementation cost (rather than personnel). Clearly, if a training analyst was examining these two approaches to reduce expenditures, different things would be considered.

You Try It

Suppose you are the training analyst at a government agency that has the responsibility for training and certifying safety inspectors. At the present time, these inspectors are trained at four regional centers where the equipment they learn to inspect is located. The agency is facing a substantial budget reduction and the director of the agency wants to know if the training budget can be reduced by consolidating the training done at the regional centers into a central facility.

You gather some facts on the present situation and discover the following:

1. There is one instructor at each of four regional centers (annual salary = $30,000).
2. About 200 students per year are taught at each center.
3. Students' room and board expenses are paid (average = $250) for the one-week course, as well as their salary (average = $500). However, they must pay for their own travel to and from the regional center (something all students gripe about).
4. The cost of operating each regional facility is $12,000 annually.
5. The annual operating and maintenance costs of the current equipment at each center is $20,000. You discover that both students and instructors are very unhappy with the equipment situation. None of the centers has all of the equipment they need to do adequate training and they claim that much of what they do have is nearly obsolete. They feel this significantly limits the effectiveness of the training.

In investigating the proposed alternative (central facility), you find out the following:

1. With a central facility, it is possible to increase the class size by team teaching and reduce the number of instructors to two. However, a training center manager will now be needed (at the same average annual salary as the instructors).
2. You ask the instructors to provide you with a "wish list" of all the equipment they would like to have. The total value of this equipment is $250,000, with an annual operating and maintenance cost of $25,000. Since this equipment has a ten-year life expectancy, its annual purchase cost is $25,000. Thus, annual equipment costs would be $25,000 + $25,000 = $50,000.
3. The agency owns an unused building that would be suitable for the training center (annual operating costs = $40,000). This facility also includes a residence so that no room and board expenses will be incurred by the students. However, it will be necessary to pay their

travel expenses and this is estimated to be $250 per student. (Students would still be paid their salary for the week as before.)
4. The current training course and materials will need to be revised due to the new equipment. This will involve an analysis ($15,000), design and development work ($30,000), and materials costs ($2,000). In addition, an evaluation will need to be done to ensure that the revised course is as effective as the previous one. This will cost $10,000.

On the basis of the information above, will the agency save money by switching to a central training facility? Follow the steps outlined in Figure 3-6 and complete a resource requirements matrix for both the existing and the proposed approach. Compare the total costs to see if the proposed approach saves money. When you have worked through the problem, check your conclusion with the one in the back of the book. *No peeking!*

For each approach to be compared:

    1.   Identify all resources required for each stage of the training cycle. Be sure they are in the same units (i.e., per year, per course, etc.).

    2.   Compute the cost of each resource for all cells of the matrix.

    3.   Sum the costs in all cells to obtain the total cost.

Complete this procedure for each approach to be compared.

Figure 3-6   Using the Resource Requirements Model

Chapter Four
Life Cycle Costs

The resource requirements models described in the previous chapter provide a way of comparing the costs of two or more different training approaches at a given point in time. However, it is often the case that a valid comparison can be made only by taking into account the entire life cycle of the training system. In this chapter you will learn about a model that allows comparison of the *relative* costs of two or more training approaches over some selected period of time. Although life cycle models could be used to compute absolute costs, they are typically used for comparative purposes.

Training System Dynamics

The four major phases of the training system life cycle were briefly described in Chapter One: R&D, startup, operational period, and transition period (see Figure 4–1). The R&D phase involves the exploration of new training techniques, technology, or methodology. One of the considerations here is that some of the approaches explored will turn out to

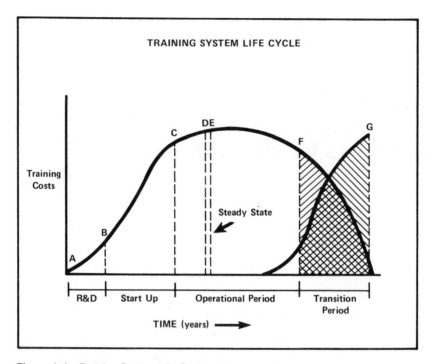

Figure 4-1 Training System Life Cycle

be dead ends, or at least not feasible for practical purposes. The cost of such unsuccessful innovations is generally written off as an R&D loss, although in some organizations the costs of such unsuccessful efforts must be borne by those that are successful. In this situation, the cost justification for a successful training innovation must not only cover its own R&D costs, but all efforts carried on under a certain program or research activity.

The amount of money spent on training R&D varies considerably. The U.S. Department of Defense conducts a great deal of training R&D, most of it focused on new technologies and training devices (i.e., equipment simulators). On the other hand, most major corporations spend relatively little on training R&D, preferring to let universities and the Department of Defense identify promising innovations for them. Because of this conservative approach, business and industry are often slow to take advantage of training improvements. Considering the relatively large sums of money that are typically invested in a large-scale training program, skimping on R&D studies is really a case of being penny-wise and pound-foolish.

At some point (usually after a successful tryout or pilot project), the decision will be made to implement the new approach on a full-scale basis. This decision should be based on some sort of evidence that the new approach will meet certain desired training goals and a favorable cost/benefits analysis. In fact, this is the place that you might develop a life cycle cost model. Note that the progression from R&D to startup may be gradual or staggered rather than abrupt. This, you may go from a pilot project to a trial implementation with a small number of students, followed by more courses or programs. Indeed, one of the reasons for doing a life cycle analysis is to determine what kind of transition from an old approach to a new approach produces in the best cost/benefits results. (We will look at an example of this problem later in this chapter.)

Once startup activities for a new approach are underway, costs rise sharply as new resources required (i.e., instructors, equipment, facilities) are acquired or new materials are developed. One of the major cost considerations associated with this startup period is the amortization of one-time equipment or facility costs, or materials development costs over the expected lifetime of the training approach. Thus, if video cassette units are purchased to be used as part of a training program and they have an expected lifetime of six years, their costs can be amortized over this period. However, the cassettes themselves may only have a lifetime of three years for the expected usage level. This means that their costs can only be amortized over a three-year period and they will need to be replaced halfway during the lifetime of the video cassette player. To make this example even more realistic, suppose the instruction on the video cassette needs revising every eighteen months. This means that the instructional development and materials required for this revision process are amortized over an eighteen-month period and that the cassettes will have to be re-recorded halfway through their lifetime. (This is just a sample of the complexity that can occur in a large-scale training system!)

The training approach is in its operational period when it is fully implemented. Because of the dynamics of training systems, it is sometimes difficult to tell that the implementation phase has been reached. For example, it is typical that some courses or components that were initially planned will never actually be implemented or are discontinued relatively early. Furthermore, there will always be things that were not planned but need to be added after full-scale implementation is underway. The point is that even after a training approach has reached the operational period, there will normally be a considerable amount of flux and change.

Once it has reached the operational period, a training approach becomes the baseline to which new or alternative approaches are now compared. In other words, yesterday's innovation becomes today's status quo. During the operational period (which may last from several months to many years, depending upon the nature of the organization and the training), training costs should not change substantially.

At some point, a better approach will be found and a decision made to replace the existing approach with the new one. In most cases, it is not possible to simply dump one approach and replace it with another over night. Changing over normally takes a period of months or years while old training equipment or materials are replaced by new ones or new techniques are used. During this transition period, some students may be taught with the old approach, while others get the new approach.

Even in cases where the new approach simply involves one curriculum replacing another, the effects of the old curriculum in terms of the way trainees perform will still persist until they are retrained with the new curriculum or replaced by employees who have been. (This is called the "generation effect" of a training program.)

For example, suppose that an engine manufacturer introduces a new type of solid state engine that requires electronics knowledge to repair—knowledge that current mechanics do not have. The necessary course is developed and implemented so that all new mechanics being trained receive this knowledge. However, there are thousands of mechanics who must be retrained. Until this has been done, there exists a transition period in the training system where new mechanics are learning one thing (repairing the new engine) but older mechanics are performing another (repairing the old engines). As you might realize from this example, any large-scale training system will typically have quite a number of courses or programs in a transition period at any one time.

During transition periods, the costs spent on the existing approach should be dropping off sharply as it is abandoned. At the same time, the startup costs for the new approach are increasing sharply. The total training costs during a transition period include the combined costs for both old and new approaches, and theoretically are highest at the crossover point where the new approach is half-implemented (i.e., the old and new approaches are being used equally). From this crossover point, total costs start to decline until they reach the level of operational costs for the new approach (see Figure 4–2).

Since this transition period can be the most expensive phase of a training system, it is essential to develop an implementation plan that minimizes the transition period costs. It is important to realize that the shortest transition period may not necessarily be the least expensive. By

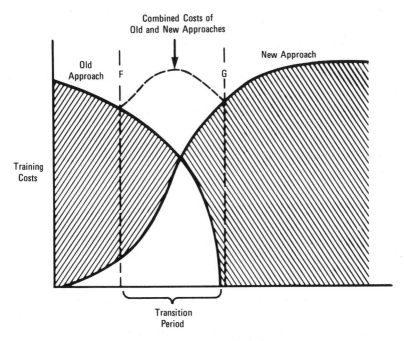

Figure 4-2 Training Costs During Transition Period

stretching out the transition period, it may not be necessary to replace as much equipment or materials. Rather, new equipment and revised materials can replace old when they would have needed replacing anyway. Similarly, instead of retraining employees, it may be possible with a long enough transition period to simply replace them as they leave due to attrition or retirement. On the other hand, in cases where the new training approach results in substantial operating cost savings over the previous approach, the shortest transition period possible may produce the best overall cost savings despite high replacement or retraining costs. We will look at an example shortly that illustrates the cost considerations of transition periods.

Discussions about the length of transition periods are affected by things other than costs, of course. It may be desirable, for organizational reasons, to make the changeover from the one approach to another as quickly (or perhaps, as slowly) as possible. A life cycle cost analysis could show that a one-year transition is optimal, but it may be that new equipment or facilities cannot be acquired or readied for two years. You should always keep in mind that cost models produce information to be considered in making decisions—at times other information may be more important.

In any large-scale training system as would be found in a major corporation, government agency, or the military, there will be many training programs in different phases of the training cycle. At any given time, there may be five programs in operational phases, one in startup, two in transition, and three R&D projects. The total training system life cycle costs will reflect the changing costs of these programs projected over some planning period such as five or ten years.

In addition to these long-term, macroscopic dynamics, training systems have short-term, microscopic dynamics, too. In projecting the expected costs of a training program, it is often necessary to estimate the resources needed over a period of weeks, months, or years. Thus, it will be necessary to estimate how many instructors, developers, classrooms, study rooms, workbooks, slide projectors, etc., will be needed at any particular time in the training system. For example, suppose the problem is to determine how many computer-based flight simulators an airline will need for its pilot training program for a new aircraft. Figure 4–3 shows the expected student loads during the first year, based upon the

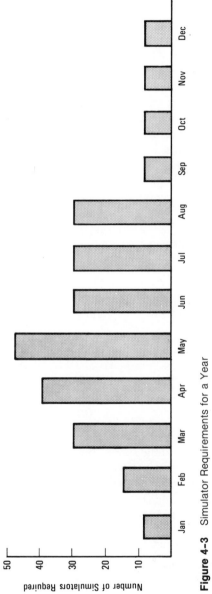

Figure 4-3 Simulator Requirements for a Year

number of pilots needed for the aircraft being delivered and put into service. The simplest solution would be to order fifty simulators and be able to handle the loads at the peak levels. The problem with this decision is that the simulators are worth about $500,000 each, and fifty simulators are only needed for two months—the rest of the year thirty would be adequate for the peak load. Thus, a training analyst would expend some effort into rescheduling or restructuring the simulator training such that no more than thirty simulators would be needed in any one month.

This kind of resource scheduling problem is very common in the planning of training systems. However, resource scheduling is hardly a problem unique to the training domain. Virtually all organizations must schedule resources, whether it is trucks to deliver products to customers or the availability of accountants at tax time. Thus, short-term cost dynamics of training systems, as important as they are, are not discussed further in this book. They are an appropriate topic for a book on business management, not cost/benefits analysis in training systems.

Life Cycle Cost Equations

To compute life cycle costs, the following equation is used:

$$
\begin{array}{cccc}
\text{Total} & \text{Total} & \text{Total} & \text{Total} \\
\text{Life Cycle} = \text{R\&D/Startup} + \text{Transition} + \text{Steady State} \\
\text{Costs} & \text{Costs} & \text{Costs} & \text{Costs} \\
(t) & & (n) & (m)
\end{array}
$$

In words, for a given life cycle of t months or years, the total training system costs are equal to the sum of the total R&D/startup costs, the total transition costs over the transition period of n months or years, and the total steady state costs over an operational period of m months or years. Since the R&D and startup activities take place during the transition period, the period of the life cycle (t) equals the sum of $n + m$.

Clearly, the length of the transition and operational periods will affect the total life cycle cost. For example, consider a training system that involves converting slides, audiotapes, and videotapes to videodisc for packaging multimedia training programs. The total R&D and startup cost is $150,000; the total transition cost (which involves the purchase of videodisc players and conversion of all existing materials to videodisc) is $250,000, and the operational cost will be $90,000 annually (including operating and maintenance costs on the equipment).

Suppose that the life cycle of this program is fixed at six years. If the transition period is three years, the steady state period will be $6 - 3 = 3$ years. Thus, the total life cycle cost will be:

$150,000 + $250,000 + ($90,000 \times 3 = $270,000) = $670,000.

However, if the transition period is two years, the steady state period will be four years, resulting in the following total life cycle cost:

$150,000 + $250,000 + ($90,000 \times 4 = $360,000) = $760,000.

According to this example, a shorter transition period will result in a greater total life cycle cost. However, this example has a missing piece. If, during the steady state phase of the new program, money is being saved over the previous approach, the longer the operational period, the more money saved. The total life cycle cost savings between two approaches are given by the following equation:

Total Life Cycle = Total Life Cycle Costs − Total Life Cycle Costs
Cost Savings   Approach A   Approach B

which amounts to the following equation when one of the approaches is the existing training approach:

Total   Total   Total   Total   Total
Life Cycle = Steady State − R&D/ + Transition + Steady State
Cost Savings Costs (Old)   Startup Costs   Costs (New)
    (t) (t) Costs (n) (m)

The total life cycle cost savings for a period t, are the total R&D/startup, transition, and steady state costs for the new approach, subtracted from the total steady state costs for the old (i.e., existing) approach.

Now back to the example. Suppose that the total steady state costs of the slide/tape approach were $150,000 per year. For a life cycle period of six years, the old system would cost $900,000. With a transition period of three years, the new system will cost $670,000, for a total cost savings of $330,000 over the six-year life cycle. With the two-year transition period, the total cost savings is $240,000. Note, however, that the two-year transition period, which has an operational period of four years, results in a steady state cost savings of ($150,000 × 4 = $600,000) − ($90,000 × 4 = $360,000) = $240,000; while the three-year transitional period, with an operational period of three years, results in a steady state cost savings of only ($150,000 × 3 = $450,000) − ($90,000 × 3 = $270,000) = $180,000. Thus, for the six-year life cycle period selected, the three-year transition period results in a greater total life cycle cost savings than the two-year transition period, but the two-year transition period results in greater steady state cost savings.

To summarize, the duration of the transition and the operational periods can affect the nature of the cost savings that result in the life cycle of a training program. In general, the shorter the transition period and the longer the steady state period, the greater the cost savings to be realized. However, in cases such as the preceding example, a longer transition period may maximize savings for a particular life cycle period. Sometimes the R&D and startup costs of a new training approach will outweight the savings expected from a reasonable operational period and, hence, indicate that in terms of life cycle costs, the new approach is not cost effective. In the example just given, the R&D, startup, and transition costs totaled $400,000; however, the annual operational savings were only $60,000. This means that it would take almost seven years before the actual savings exceeded the initial "sunk" costs, even though relative cost savings over the old approach would be generated much earlier.

An Example: Product Training

The sales and service training associated with new products is a good candidate for life cycle cost analysis, since most major products (e.g., automobiles, aircraft, computers, washing machines, etc.) have a relatively long lifetime during which training must be available.

In the usual case, when the new product is announced, the majority (if not all) of the sales and service force must be trained as quickly as possible. Following this initial training period, the training must be available for the lifetime of the product for new employees—even though this may be a relatively small number of employees over a long period. Incidentally, the considerations associated with new product training are very similar to those associated with new weapons systems training in the military or operator/maintenance training for a new piece of manufacturing equipment in an industrial setting.

In our example, all new product training is currently done by videotapes, which are distributed to each branch office a few weeks before the product announcement date and are kept there for subsequent training of new employees. Two one-hour tapes are made for each new product—a sales tape and a service tape. These tapes are watched in a group session with all salespersons or service technicians and their managers present.

There are seventy-five branch offices in the organization and each has a videotape system that initially costs $2,000 each. Annual operating and maintenance costs on the system average $100 per year and the system has an average life expectancy of five years before replacement is needed. Of the seventy-five branches, five have had their systems for four years, twenty have had their systems for three years, and fifty for two years. The first five players were part of the R&D on this approach (which replaced centralized classroom training), and the remaining seventy were introduced during a two-year startup/transition period.

The average cost of making a sales or service videotape is $60,000, including all analysis, design, and production work. The duplication and distribution costs of each tape sent to a branch are $20. There are an average of three product announcements made each year, which means six tapes (three sales and three service) are made annually.

One of the problems with the current approach to product training is that the training department has no control over when the tapes are initially viewed—it is the responsibility of the branch manager to schedule the training meetings. While most managers schedule them at the time of announcement, some do not hold them until well after announcement date and, consequently, their sales and service representations lack the product knowledge they should have. Other problems include the lack of opportunity to get knowledgeable answers to questions about the products during the training session and the shortness of the training.

When the organization decided to invest in a satellite teleconferencing system that would place receivers at each branch office, the training department was asked to explore possible uses of this system in its training activities. The use of teleconferencing for new product training seemed like a good idea since it would mean that all branches would get their training about the same time and there would be an opportunity for the product designers to answer questions. A pilot project was initiated involving training at five branches for a new product at a cost of $150,000. This pilot effort was so successful that an immediate decision was made to replace the videotape training with teleconferencing. One of the factors affecting the decision was a favorable life cycle cost comparison (along with data showing improved sales and service performance on the new product).

Let's examine the life cycle cost analysis. The teleconferencing approach involves the installation of receivers and necessary studio facilities at each branch for a one-time cost of $12,000 per branch. Thus, total installation cost for all seventy-five branches is $900,000. In addition, another $60,000 is needed to set up the transmitting station resulting in a total equipment cost of $960,000 for the teleconferencing system. This equipment is to be amortized over a three-year period, i.e., $320,000 per year. The annual operating and maintenance costs are an additional $40,000 per year, making the total annual expense $360,000. Since the training department has been allocated twenty-five percent of the time (sixty days) available, it will pay $90,000. Product training will use fifteen of the sixty days available, so the total share of the equipment cost for product training is $22,500.

Each teleconference for a new product will be split into a morning for sales training and the afternoon for service training. The pilot research showed that about fifteen branches could be handled simultaneously at each teleconference (a total of about sixty participants). Thus, the same teleconference will have to be repeated on five days to cover all seventy-five branches. The cost of using the satellite is $10,000 per day, so the cost of each product training effort will be 5 × $10,000 = $50,000. Since there are three new products per year, the annual teleconferencing cost will be $150,000.

The development of each teleconference will cost $20,000 (covering both sales and service). This covers the design and development, the presentations, and all materials. It also covers the time of those giving the teleconference.

To handle product training after the initial training session, the teleconferences (which are in video form) will be edited into three-hour video cassette programs and distributed to each branch, just as the previous videotapes were. This editing activity will average $10,000 per tape for a total of $60,000 for the six video cassettes that will be made for the three new products. The duplication and distribution costs are basically the same as in the existing approach: $20 per cassette or a total of $9,000 per year to send two to each branch for each of three new products.

Besides the costs of the tape duplication and distribution, there are other costs that will be the same across both old and new approaches and can be treated as "wash" costs in the comparison. This includes costs such as the sales literature and service manuals that must be sent to all branches and the time of the participants at the branches (which is a training cost).

The anticipated life cycle of the teleconferencing approach is six years. Installation of the receivers and studios at each branch will be done within a period of a few months, and so there is no need for a transition period as far as the teleconferencing equipment is concerned. However, there will be a transition period during which the new video cassette players replace the existing videotape players. The old videotape players will be kept for product training on previous products, many of which will have lifetimes that last well after the videotape program is phased out. (Note that since the videotape machines would have needed replacing by the end of the third year of the new program anyway, they can be considered a "wash cost" for the comparison.)

Let's calculate the annual life cycle costs for the previous (videotape-based) approach:

Production of videotapes:	6 × $60,000	=	$360,000
Duplication/distribution:	6 × 75 × $20	=	9,000
Maintenance of players:	75 × $100	=	7,500
		Total	$376,500

The annual life cycle costs for the new (teleconference-based) approach are:

Equipment costs (including maintenance):			$ 22,500
Satellite usage:	3 × $50,000	=	150,000
Development cost:	3 × $20,000	=	60,000
Editing cost:	6 × $10,000	=	60,000
Duplication/distribution:	6 × 75 × $20	=	9,000
Maintenance of players (cassette):	75 × $100	=	7,500
		Total	$309,000

49

This annual cost is for the first three years. For each subsequent year of the life cycle, the annual cost will exclude the equipment cost (i.e., $22,500) and thus be $286,500. So we have:

Total   Total   Total   Total
Life Cycle = R&D + Startup + Steady State
Costs   Costs   Costs   Costs
(6 years)   (3 years) (3 years)

Total
Life Cycle = $150,000 + (3 × $309,000) + (3 × $286,500)
Costs   =   1,936,500

Total
Life Cycle = (6 × $376,500) − $1,936,500 = $322,500
Savings
(6 years)

Thus, the total life cycle cost savings for a six-year period between the current videotape-based product training approach and the proposed teleconference-based approach is $322,500. In fact, the new approach would generate a cost savings of $52,500 at the end of the third year. The annual steady state cost savings for each year of the operational approach is ($376,500 − $286,500) = $90,000.

We are not quite done with our example yet, since we still need to calculate some transition costs. As you will recall, video cassette players will be installed into the branches for viewing all new product training that results from teleconferences. The plan is to leave the old videotape players in the branches for viewing existing product videotapes. However, if we do leave the videotape players in the branches, we will have to pay maintenance costs for both the new cassette players and the old videotape players. Alternatively, we could simply convert all of the existing videotapes to video cassettes and get rid of all the videotape players. Let's see which transition plan is most cost-effective.

At the end of the first year, there will be twenty-five sets (i.e., one for service and one for sales) of product training tapes still in use. At the end of the second year, twenty sets will be in use, and at the end of the third year, ten sets. The duplication and distribution cost for putting two videotapes onto a single video cassette and shipping them is $25.

If we simply convert all of the existing videotapes to video cassettes at the beginning of the first year, the cost would be:

(25 tapes) × ($25 each) × (75 branches) = $46,875

If instead, we wait until the end of the first year, the cost would be:

(20 tapes) × ($25 each) × (75 branches) = $37,500

However, we must pay maintenance cost on the videotape players (75 × $100) = $7,500 as well, making the total costs for this alternative:

$37,500 + 7,500 = $45,000

A third alternative would be to wait until the end of the second year with the following conversion cost:

(10 tapes) × ($25 each) × (75 branches) = $18,750

However, we have maintenance costs from two years to add (i.e., $7,500 × 2 = $15,000), giving us a total of $18,750 + $15,000 = $33,750 for this alternative.

On the basis of these calculations, it appears that the most cost-effective plan is to wait until the end of the second year before converting all of the remaining videotapes to video cassettes. This will save $46,875 − $33,750 = $13,125 over the cost of conversion at the beginning of the first year. Thus, we have found that a two-year transition period from videotape to video cassette makes the best sense in this example. (We should now go back and add $33,750 as transition costs to our total life cycle costs for the new approach, thereby reducing the total savings to $288,750.)

Other Life Cycle Cost Considerations

An economist or accountant reading this chapter would surely snicker. The investment of large sums of money over a number of years is subject to all kinds of financial complexities, which have been completely ignored so far in this chapter. For example, in amortizing equipment purchases over a number of years, a simple straight-line method has been used where the total sum is divided by the number of years to produce the annual cost. However, amortization would rarely be calculated this way in reality. For one thing, *depreciation* on capital investments (i.e., equipment, buildings) would usually be taken into account. Inflation rates and interest on capital investments might also be taken into consideration. When equipment or facilities are replaced, they often have a *surplus value.* It is also likely that cost savings calculated for future years would be *discounted,* i.e., converted from future value to present value (or the reverse). Thus, $1,000 saved in three years with an annual discount rate of twelve percent amounts to $712 today. Suffice it to say that an economist or accountant would typically be involved in computing life cycle costs in any organization or agency that does a lot of long-term planning. On the other hand, the addition of these considerations usually makes the figures more precise but seldom changes the nature of the outcomes. If you can make a strong case for the cost effectiveness of a training approach using the relatively simple methods outlined in this chapter, they are likely to stand up under the more sophisticated analysis of a financial expert.

In the introductory chapter, the terms *cost reduction, cost avoidance,* and *value-added savings* were explained. The kinds of cost savings discussed in this and the previous chapter are typically based on cost reduction or cost avoidance. In Chapter Three, there was an example involving customer relations training to reduce customer complaints. Presumably, sufficiently disgruntled customers take their business elsewhere; customer relations training saves us money we might have lost due to customers leaving. This is a cost avoidance situation, which we could quantify if we wanted to by estimating the value of accounts lost due to unhappy customers. The centralized versus distributed product training in that chapter is a case of savings due to cost reduction. The decentralized training saved $34,000 annually over the centralized approach.

However, the decentralized training in that example also results in some other benefits: product training is standardized for all employees, training can be given to all stores at the same time, and half of the time of the trainer was released. These are value-added benefits. The fact that product training is standardized for all employees means that we can count on all employees having had the necessary training to sell the products. (Of course, we cannot assume it was equally effective with everyone—some people may have slept through the videotapes). The fact that the training is given to all stores at the same time should mean that all stores can begin selling the product immediately. Finally, the fact that the new approach required only half of the trainer's time presumably means that the trainer was able to do two such projects at the same time instead of just one (hence doubling his or her productivity).

The new product training example in this chapter also shows cost reduction and value added kinds of cost savings. The money saved by using the teleconferences rather than the videotapes is a cost reduction. In addition, the sales and service representatives got longer training and an opportunity to ask the product designers questions about the new products. Furthermore, the training department was able to ensure that the training was given at the time of product announcement. All of these results are value-added benefits.

It is possible (although sometimes difficult) to associate dollar amounts with value-added benefits. For example, if we know that a certain number of stores or employees do not get around to completing their training on a new product, we can calculate a *lost opportunity* cost. Suppose that our sales data show that all sales representatives can sell at least three of the new products per week while making their regular calls. If there are six branches with a total of twenty-four sales representatives who do not complete the product training until one week has elapsed since the announcement date, we have lost potential sales of $3 \times 24 = 72$ units. If these are $10 widgets, then this is not much of a lost opportunity cost; however, if it is a $2,000 piece of equipment, then we have lost quite a bit (e.g., $140,000).

Many types of value-added benefits have second or third order effects. Thus, a customer who is particularly pleased with the product or service of a company may not only buy more from that company, but may promote the company by praising it to friends (good old "word of mouth" advertising) or invest in company stock. An operator who learns to operate a machine properly not only produces more finished units, but may reduce the machine's downtime and maintenance costs. A manager who is trained in how to delegate responsibility to subordinates, thereby preparing them for management roles, may save the corporation considerable costs in terms of management training, employee turnover or attrition, and recruitment/selection. Although we often tend to forget the meaning of the term *system*, in a training system all components are interrelated and interdependent. Benefits that affect one component tend to propagate throughout the system. Thus, while we can put dollar amounts on value-added benefits, it would be much more useful if we could see the effects of a benefit on the overall system. In the next chapter we shall look at a model that allows us to do this.

You Try It

Here's your chance to try your hand at life cycle costing. Got your calculator ready? The training manager of a large corporaton becomes convinced that a computer-managed, self-study approach could reduce the length of a management training program that is currently taught via the traditional classroom/lecture approach.

The manager funds a pilot project (cost: $32,000) which converts about four hours of lecture into a multimedia self-study format. The data from the study show that the managers average about three hours to complete this instruction in the self-study format. On the basis of this data (and an examination of such systems already in use at other organizations), the manager concludes that the current 4½ day course can be reduced to 3½ days by converting it totally to computer-managed self-study.

By reducing the length of the course by a day, an average cost savings of $150 per manager results for salaries. In addition, a day of room and board is saved ($50). Thus, $200 is saved for each manager by reducing the course length by one day. Approximately 1,800 managers a year attend this course.

To implement the self-study approach, it is necessary to develop new multimedia materials from the existing lecture materials, modify two classrooms into a multimedia learning center, and acquire the necessary equipment. The facility modifications will cost $40,000. The equipment needed totals $60,000, and this would be amortized over three years. In addition, there would be yearly operating and maintenance costs of $6,000.

There are two possible choices for development. The manager can contract with the company that conducted the pilot study for the development of the new curricula at a total cost of $180,000. Alternatively, the work could be done by the corporation's internal training development group at a cost of $120,000. However, the contractor could do the work in six months, while the internal group would require a year. In addition, a supplemental instructor must be hired (annual salary:

For each approach to be compared:

1. Identify all of the resource costs associated with the existing approach.

2. Identify all of the resource costs or cost savings associated with the proposed approach. This includes all R&D costs, start-up costs, transition costs, and steady state costs.

3. Determine any "wash" costs which would be the same in the existing and proposed approach.

4. Establish the expected lifetime of the proposed approach, as well as start-up/transition period. You will probably want to examine a range of possible durations.

5. Compute the life cycle costs of the existing and proposed approaches for the same period(s).

6. Compute the life cycle cost savings for each period you are examining.

Figure 4-4 Using the Life Cycle Cost Model

$36,000) while the new curriculum is being designed, so that the existing instructors can work with the developers to create the new curricula. (After the new course is in place, the same number of instructors would be involved.)

If the life cycle of the new self-study approach is assumed to be five years, what are the life cycle cost savings over the present approach? What is the best transition period: six months or one year? What are the savings during the operational period? Figure 4-4 summarizes the steps you need to follow.

Chapter Five

Benefits Analysis

In the previous two chapters, we have been looking at models that basically address training efficiency rather than effectiveness. Using the resource requirements or life cycle models to compare different training approaches is based on an assumption of equal effectiveness. If two approaches are assumed to be equally effective and one can be shown to cost less, then it is more efficient.

However, suppose you are more interested in improving effectiveness rather than efficiency. You want to find an approach that will result in better training outcomes for the same amount of money as an existing approach. Or, you may be concerned with achieving better training results even if it costs you more. You want a method for comparing the relative benefits of two or more training approaches at a given level of costs. This chapter describes such a method—benefits analysis.

Benefits analysis can also help you capture the costs of inadequate training. For example, the costs of not adequately training a commercial jet pilot in terms of a single plane crash due to pilot error are tremendous. Similarly, the costs of not properly training an oil rig roughneck on safety procedures are also tremendous in terms of a well blowout or fire. In the sales domain, the costs of inadequate training are lost sales. In management training, the consequences of inadequate training are poor decisions and planning—ultimately leading to reduced profits and success. Overtime, high turnover, poor morale, additional employees, and excessive equipment maintenance are other consequences typically associated with inadequate training. Being able to identify the training approach that prevents inadequate training is tantamount to finding a training approach that provides better training.

Causal Relations in Training Systems

The benefits analysis model described in this chapter is based on a network of causal relationships between training system attributes and benefits (see Figure 5–1). As explained in Chapter Two, the training system attributes are linked to certain training outcomes (such as student completion time, duration of retention, development time, etc.), which in turn are linked to certain operational outcomes (such as job proficiency, safety records, sales volume, etc.). Figure 5–2 lists some common training system attributes and outcomes.

A unique set of attributes and outcomes are developed for each training approach and situation being analyzed. The attributes are derived from the properties of the training approaches being compared. Thus, if we are comparing two types of media approaches (e.g., slide/tape versus videotape), then the attributes that distinguish these approaches (e.g., presentation capabilities, development and revision requirements, etc.) are the ones we are interested in. On the other hand, if we are comparing two different training delivery systems (e.g., classroom lectures versus computer-based instruction), the attributes will need to be selected to allow comparison on the characteristics expected to differentially affect training outcomes (e.g., in this case, interactive or data collection capabilities).

The identification of the training outcomes depends on what outcomes we expect to be affected by the comparison being made, as well as the outcomes that are known to be important in the particular training system under study. For example, if we were comparing an approach that involved video versus one that did not, we would be interested in the

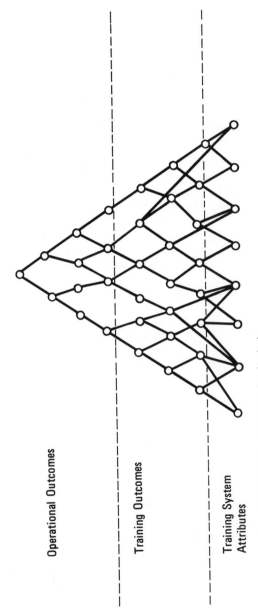

Operational Outcomes

Training Outcomes

Training System
Attributes

Figure 5-1 Casual Model Underlying Benefits Analysis

TRAINING SYSTEM ATTRIBUTES

- Structure of Materials
- Student Capacity
- Presentation Capabilities
- Testing Capabilities
- Interactive Capabilities
- Data Collection Capabilities
- Individualization Capability

- Development Requirements
- Revision Requirements
- Instructor Requirements
- Administrative Requirements
- Maintenance Requirements
- Operating Range
- Instructional Strategies

TRAINING OUTCOMES

- Student Throughput (Number of Graduates)
- Student Completion Time
- Testing Time
- Development Time
- Retention Period
- Motivation/Attitude Change

- Achievement Level (Accuracy, Speed)
- Revision Time
- Attrition/Failure Rate
- Absentee Rate
- Accident Rates (Training)
- Amount of Practice

OPERATIONAL OUTCOMES

- Production Rate/Quality
- Sales Volume
- Equipment Failure Rates
- Job Turnover Rates

- Quality/Speed of Service
- Accident Rates (On the Job)
- Job Proficiency
- Customer or Employee Satisfaction

Figure 5-2 Training Attributes and Outcomes

motivation/attitudinal outcomes, since we know that video tends to have affective (rather than cognitive) instructional effects. If we were dealing with a training system in which the dropout rate has been a problem, attrition rate would be an outcome of interest to us.

Finally, we must identify a set of relevant operational outcomes. These should derive from the basic goals of the training program or mission statement of the organization. Thus, in sales training, the change in sales volume as a consequence of training is obviously our most important operational outcome. On the other hand, many kinds of training have multiple outcomes. For example, the outcomes we are interested in as a consequence of training a person how to operate a lawnmower are safety, minimal equipment failure (i.e., operator caused), and customer satisfaction.

Once the initial set of training system attributes and outcomes has been specified, the next step is to identify relationships. (Actually, you already used implicit relationships to isolate attributes and outcomes.) A relationship between an attribute and a training outcome or between a training outcome and an operational outcome represents an inference about a causal link between the former and the latter. For example, if you identify a link between the attribute, presentation capability (e.g., color), and the training outcome, retention period, you are hypothesizing that a certain way of presenting instructional materials will produce a change in the amount of student retention obtained (e.g., increase or decrease it). Similarly, if you identify a link between the training outcome, retention period, and the operational benefit, sales volume, you are inferring that a change in the amount of student retention obtained will affect the sales volume obtained. To put this example in concrete terms, the hypothesis is that the use of color in product training will increase the students' retention of product details, allowing them to do a better sales job.

Refer again to Figure 5–1. As you can see from this figure, there may be several levels of attributes, training outcomes, and operational outcomes. Thus, the major category of attribute may be presentation capabilities, but that may encompass a set of more specific properties of the training approach (e.g., color, speed, image resolution, motion, etc.). Similarly, a number of specific training outcomes may link to a more general one (e.g., achievement level, attitude change, absentee rate—all affecting failure rate). And major operational outcomes may likewise be composed of subsets. For example, increased sales volume may be a function of improved product knowledge, improved sales techniques, and improved interpersonal skills.

The number of levels and complexity of the causal model are determined by the scope of the training system or program analyzed and the depth of the analysis. In essence, when you develop the causal model required for benefits analysis, you are developing a partial simulation of your training system or program.

Once you have developed the causal model, you can then change the attributes to correspond to different training approaches and see their effects on the training and operational outcomes in terms of the relationships you have defined. This is done by assigning coefficients to the causal links between each pair of attributes and outcomes or outcomes and outcomes. These coefficients range from −1 to +1 and represent the estimated amount of variance accounted for by one variable or the other. A coefficient less than 0 represents a negative effect (e.g., multimedia capability increases revision time required), and a coefficient greater than 0 represents a positive effect (e.g., modularized lesson design reduces revision time). If it was determined that the particular type of multimedia capability being considered increases revision time by a factor of four times, the coefficient would be −.25. If it was determined that modular lesson design cut revision time in half, the coefficient would be +.5.

You should be careful not to automatically assume that a positive coefficient means the effect of A on B is a benefit and a negative coefficient means a disbenefit. For example, in the preceding example, the coefficient of .5 between modular design and revision time did mean a benefit. However, consider the effect of the attribute, interactive capability, on the outcome, student completion time. Assume there is a coefficient of +.2 between these two. This is interpreted as meaning that the interactive capabilities of a training approach increase the student completion time by 20 percent. However, under most circumstances, increases in student completion time are not seen as benefits but, instead, drawbacks. Thus, this positive coefficient does not signify a benefit—at least as far as the effect of interaction on student completion time is concerned. However, the coefficient of +.5 between interaction and amount of practice indicates that this capability increases the amount of practice by 50 percent—a benefit.

How do you determine these coefficients? They may come from a number of sources. First of all, you can sit back in your armchair and make them up. As an improvement on solitary "armchair" speculation, you could convene a meeting of experts and use the results of this collective wisdom. (There are techniques, such as Delphi, that could be used for this purpose.) You can take your coefficients from the results of experiments or past results reported in the literature. Or, if a particular link is very critical, you could do some experiments to find out how much one thing affects another. In short, there is a range of possible ways to determine the value of the coefficients, each with different degrees of validity. You will have to select the method that is appropriate for the importance of the benefits analysis you are conducting. If you were conducting a benefits analysis to help make a multimillion dollar decision, you would want your coefficients to be based on as solid data as possible. Theoretically, it is possible to determine the value of each coefficient in the model experimentally. However, with any reasonably sized causal model, this would not be feasible. In general, the coefficients are derived from a variety of sources, depending upon what information is available and the criticality of the links. There will be some links for which you are content with "armchaired" coefficients, others you will want to base on group judgments or past data, and a few really important coefficients may have to be determined empirically.

Before we go on, let's deal with a concern that often arises at this point. It can be expressed as "How do you expect me to take that model seriously? You made it all up!" This is absolutely true. The causal model is completely "made up." All of the relationships and their coefficients are inferences or assumptions about what affects what (and how much) in a particular training system. However, this is no different from our normal practice of making decisions—we make lots of inferences and assumptions. The difference in the case of benefits analysis is that we have made all of our inferences and assumptions *explicit* (painfully so) so that they can examined and challenged. In fact, this is one of the great strengths of the benefits model—it serves as a means of documenting and discussing your ideas about how a training system works. If someone else sees a relationship differently, she or he can point it out and more information can be collected to settle the dispute. Without a benefits analysis model, most of the detailed assumptions made in cost/benefits decisions are kept in our head and are not subject to analysis. Consequently, we are not able to really understand how to improve training system effectiveness. (Instead, we just argue a lot.) Benefits analysis is a methodology that helps make subjective decisions a good deal more objective.

Back to the model. So far we have discussed how to put coefficients on the relationships between variables. However, recall that the purpose of the model is to allow us to compare two or more training approaches. We do this by giving different weights to the attributes associated with each training approach we are comparing. For example, suppose that the student capacity of a new approach is judged to be about 1/3 greater than the existing approach. We would give it a weight of 1, while the existing approach would be assigned the weight of 0.67. If two approaches are considered equal on an attribute, they are both given the weight of 1. If one approach is considered to completely lack an attribute, it is given the weight of 0, while the other approach has the weight of 1. Unlike coefficients of relationships that can be negative, attribute weights must always be positive.

Where do the weights come from? They are assigned on the same basis as the coefficients—judgments, guesses, data, etc. However, the assignment of the weights is usually a much easier task than the derivation of the relationship coefficients because the training approach attributes are frequently quite tangible. For example, one approach can handle twenty students per day versus ten, or one approach has color whereas the other does not. Usually specifications about the training approaches being compared provide the information necessary to develop the weights and little further work is needed. For some comparisons, however, it is necessary to look for data or make judgments. Those who disagree with your selection of weights are always free to change them to their liking and run the analysis again. (This is true of the relationship coefficients, too.)

At this point, we have identified an initial set of attributes we wish to compare, the training and operational outcomes we think derive from these attributes, the relationships between all attributes and outcomes (with coefficients), and the relative weights of the attributes for the approaches being compared. At last, we are ready to conduct a benefits analysis!

Benefits Analysis Computation

The actual computational procedure for the benefits analysis is very simple, but you may find it difficult to grasp at first. We start with the set of attribute weights for an approach and we multiply each of these weights by the coefficients for all of the training outcomes it is linked to. This gives us a new set of derived weights for the original attributes in terms of their effect on the training outcomes. Next, we multiple each of the derived weights by the coefficients for all of the operational attributes it is linked to. This gives us a new set of derived weights for the attributes in terms of their effect on the operational outcomes. Now we repeat this whole process for a second training approach we wish to compare with the first. Once we have done this, we are able to compare the difference between the two approaches on the operational or training outcomes.

For example, suppose we were comparing the results of two training approaches that involved different types of testing (criterion-referenced versus norm-based). We are interested in whether the type of test will affect test production time. Thus, we can look at production rate and see that in the approach that used criterion-referenced testing, production was 2 percent higher. If this was the only difference between the two approaches (quite unlikely), then we could make the inference that criterion-referenced testing would improve production slightly. We will look at a more complete example shortly.

Formally, the model may be defined by:

$$O_j = \sum_i^k C_i \times O_i$$

where O_j is the jth outcome and C_i is the coefficient associated with O_i, the ith outcome or attribute. Each outcome (O_i) is represented by the summation of the set of k outcomes or attributes that affect it. As this computation is made for each successive outcome, O_j's of lower levels become the O_j's of higher levels in the causal model. The coefficients of C_i may range from -1 to $+1$, whereas the initial coefficients of O_i (the attribute weights) range from 0 to 1.

The k coefficients associated with any particular outcome need not combine to unity, since the specified outcomes may not completely account for the higher level outcome. For example, a set of outcomes, O_1, O_2, and O_3 may only account for half of outcome O_4; the remaining half being unknown or due to factors outside the training domain. This is a very important aspect of the model and benefits analysis. It allows for the normal situation where we do not know everything! Of course, we lose precision in our final computaton of outcomes because we have not accounted for all causes and relationships. On the other hand, we only get the degree of precision warranted by what we know and this is quite reasonable.

As a consequence of allowing partial causality (i.e., the coefficients do not necessarily constitute unity), the benefits analysis exhibits attenua-

65

tion of effects as the distance in the model increases from attributes to operational outcomes. Thus, an attribute or outcome may exert a strong effect at a particular level, but this effect becomes weaker at each higher level in the model due to the neutralizing influence of other outcomes. On the other hand, higher level outcomes may become quite robust due to the accumulation effects of many outcomes that affect it.

An Example: Improving Mission Readiness

At this point, the best thing to do is to look at an example that illustrates the benefits analysis computation. You should understand that in a real benefits analysis, the model is likely to consist of hundreds of outcomes and relationships, and the computations would most certainly be done by computer. In order to do the computations by hand, we will look at a very simple model, which would represent only a small piece of an actual benefits analysis model.

The example has to do with improving mission readiness (preparedness for combat) in the military. The problem is to compare two training approaches (to be explained later) and see which appears to have the greatest potential for improving mission readiness.

Mission readiness is primarily a function of two operational factors that can be affected by training: the availability of skilled weapons systems operators and the availability of operational equipment (i.e., the weapons systems). An analysis of the training system suggests that the availability of skilled operators is primarily a function of training throughput (how many operators can be trained), the job/task proficiency of the graduates, and the number lost due to attrition. Improving any one of these factors should increase the availability of skilled operators. Availability of operational equipment is primarily a function of the job/task proficiency of the maintenance technicians (and to some extent, the operators), attrition of maintenance technicians, and the ability of the maintenance technicians to remember how to repair equipment they have been trained on or learn how to repair new equipment (retraining). Note that there are many other factors outside of the training system that affect the availability of skilled operators or operational equipment. Enlistment quotas for operator jobs and deployment strategies will affect whether operators are available when and where needed. Equipment design (i.e., reliability) and parts availability are factors that will affect the availability of operational equipment. It may turn out that these factors external to the training system have stronger effects on mission readiness than the training system factors; however, we are only interested in determining what improvements can be made to the training system in this example.

Let's consider the training factors that influence the operational outcomes. Training throughput is a function of student completion time and the time required to develop and revise the training courses. Job/task proficiency is primarily a function of the amount and kind of practice that the trainees receive. Proficiency is also affected by the entry level skills of recruits, but this factor is a recruitment rather than training system consideration. Attrition is a consequence of accident rates (i.e., students are lost due to injury or dismissal) and student motivation/attitudes. Attrition is also affected by the differential between military and civilian pay scales. However, this is obviously a consideration beyond the scope of the training system. Retention/retraining is primarily a function of the amount/kind of practice. Note that retention/retraining and job/task proficiency would both be affected by another training system variable: learning strategies. However, this variable has been left out of the model for simplification.

We are now down to the training system attributes that are to be compared across the two approaches. Completion time is affected by the student capacity of the training approach (i.e., an approach that can handle more students results in higher completion times). The amount of development and revision time required is a function of the interactive capabilities of the approach, as well as the presentation capabilities. Accident rates are a function of the operating characteristics of the training equipment (i.e., how safe is it?). The operating characteristics also affect the amount and kind of practice possible. Practice is also affected by the student capacity of the approach and its interactive and presentation capabilities. Motivation/attitudes are also affected by interactive capabilities (amount of feedback received) and presentation capabilities.

Figure 5–3 illustrates the model just described. Now that the model has been developed, let's consider the two training approaches. One training approach (the current one) is to use the actual equipment for training. The alternative approach is to use a set of specially designed operator and maintenance trainers. These trainers are computer controlled and

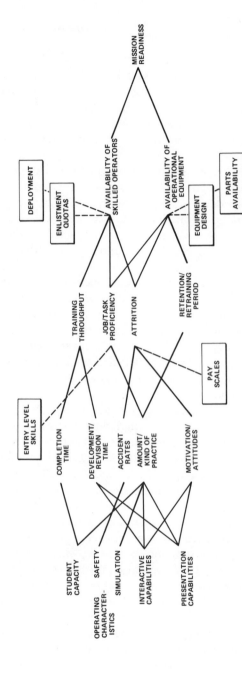

Figure 5-3 Causal Model

allow a wide range of training strategies to be implemented. Since the trainers permit most of the critical training tasks to be simulated (e.g., firing, breakdowns, etc.), they can allow a much greater degree of practice under much safer conditions. However, the trainers that are needed to replace the actual weapons system being trained upon cost about twice as much as the weapons system does. Furthermore, students prefer to train on the actual equipment rather than the trainers, even though they realize they are getting better training from the trainers. (They want the "real thing.") Given these considerations, a benefits analysis is needed to assess the merits of the two approaches.

The first thing we must do in the benefits analysis (after the model is developed) is to determine the weights of the attributes for the two approaches. As you will recall, this is a matter of rating both approaches on each attribute based upon data or judgments. Let's start with student capacity. The capacity of the set of trainers is three students simultaneously (two operators and one maintenance technician). With the actual weapons system, only one operator or one maintenance technician can be trained at once. Thus, since two weapons systems could be obtained for the cost of the set of trainers, the total student capacity is two at a time. Thus, the trainer has a 3/2 advantage over the actual equipment. We would assign the weight of 1 to the trainer and .67 to the actual equipment on the student capacity attribute.

For the operating characteristics attribute, we find that the accident rate while training on the actual equipment is .15 (i.e., fifteen accidents per one hundred students). Since there are no possibilities for accidents with the trainer, the accident rate is zero. We use .85 and 1 as the weights for operating characteristics and accident rates. The link between operating characteristics and amount/kind of practice is based on a different aspect of operating capabilities—the ability to simulate operations we would not want to actually try with the real equipment. (The obvious example is emergency procedures or maneuvers that result in loss of the weapons system.) We identify at least eight major operations that are possible on the trainer but not using the actual equipment, and assign weights of 1 to the trainer and .2 to the actual equipment on this aspect of operating characteristics and practice.

The trainers provide considerably more interactive capability (i.e., feedback possible) than the actual equipment. This is estimated to be at least a factor of two and the trainers are given a weight of 1 and the equipment is given a weight of .5.

The presentation capabilities of the system include a wide range of audiovisual features (i.e., color, motion, high resolution graphics, sound, narration, etc.). These capabilities are judged to be about one-third more instructionally effective than the actual equipment. Therefore, the weights are 1 for the trainer and .75 for the actual equipment.

Now that the weights have been determined, we can assign the coefficients on all of the relationships. Suppose that the following coefficients were derived from either data or expert judgments. The relationship between student capacity and completion time is judged to be .5, since it is the most important factor, but there are others (e.g., student motivation). The relationship between student capacity and amount of practice is considered to be .6, since it is a primary determinant of how much practice can be obtained. The relationship between the safety aspect of operating characteristics and accident rates is estimated to be .75, since other factors besides the equipment (such as fatigue) are known to affect the accident rate. The link between the simulation aspect of operating characteristics and practice is estimated to be as important as between student capacity and practice: .6. The coefficient on the relationship between interactive capabilities and development/revision time is set at −.25, since data show that interactive instruction of the kind required for trainers takes about three times longer to develop and revise. (Note that this negative coefficient signifies a disbenefit for the interactive capabilities attribute on this outcome.) The relationship between interactive capabilities and practice is set as .5, since data show that interactive capability generally leads to about twice the total amount of practice as noninteractive training. Questionnaire data show that interactive capabilities improve student motivation by a factor of 20 percent; thus, the coefficient on this link is .2. Utilization of the multimedia capabilities of the trainers increases development and revision time by a factor of at least two and the coefficient for this link is −.5. The presentation capabilities are estimated to improve the kind of practice possible by a factor of 30 percent (coefficient = .3) and student motivation by 25 percent (coefficient = .25).

Coefficients for the rest of the links between training outcomes and operational outcomes are similarly assigned and are shown in Figure 5–4.

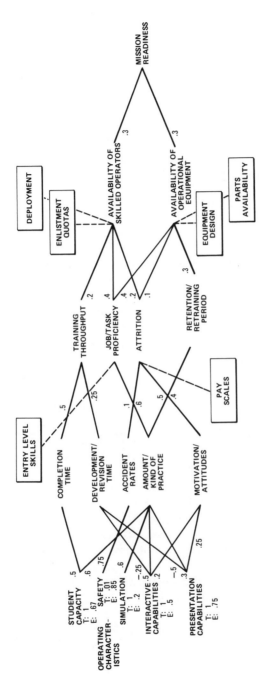

Figure 5-4 Causal Model with Initial Weights and Coefficients

71

Up until this point, we have assigned the coefficients on the basis of each link. Now we must look at the set of coefficients that influence each outcome and decide if they are appropriate in relation to each other. If any factors have coefficients that sum to more than 1, these must be standardized to coefficients that sum to less than 1. For example, the practice outcome has a set of coefficients summing to 2.0 (.6 + .6 + .5 + .3), so they must all be multiplied by .5. We decide that this set of factors together accounts for only 80 percent of the practice outcome. The original coefficients are then replaced by their standardized coefficients (now multiplied by .5 × .8). This standardization procedure can also be taken into account when the original coefficients are assigned rather than after.

One interesting thing to notice is the partial causality in the model. For example, the coefficients of the relationships between availability of operators and availability of equipment, and mission readiness, total only .6 (.3 + .3), indicating that there are other factors required to fully account for mission readiness. The partial causality is true of other outcomes in the model, as you can see for yourself.

With all of the weights and coefficients assigned, we are ready to run the model and make the comparison between the two training approaches. Figure 5–5 shows the results with the derived weights for both approaches (T for trainer; E for actual equipment) shown below each outcome.

Now we are able to draw some tentative conclusions about the two training approaches on the basis of the weights and coefficients used in the computation. The bottom line is that the use of trainers rather than the real equipment would improve mission readiness by 8 percent (.18 versus .10). This improvement is due more to improved availability of equipment (.34 versus .18) than improved availability of skilled operators (.25 versus .16). Note that there is relatively little difference between the two approaches in training throughput (.06 versus .05) or attrition (.26 versus .23). However, there is a significant difference in job/task proficiency (.48 versus .20). Interpreted loosely, these results suggest that job proficiency and retention will be twice as good using the trainers. In terms of the first order training outcomes, the most significant difference is in the amount or kind of practice possible (.80 versus .40) and the development/revision time required (−.75 versus −.51). Interpreting

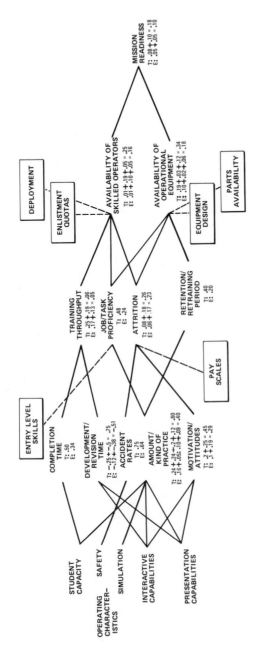

Figure 5-5 Causal Model with Derived Weights

73

these outcomes, we would conclude that the use of the trainers will substantially increase the practice students receive but also mean substantial increases in the time required to develop and revise the training.

Having drawn tentative conclusions on the basis of our original numbers, we would now try to refine the weights and coefficients that appear critical. Thus, since we have found the relationships between attributes and practice to be quite important, as well as practice with the second-order training outcomes (i.e., retention/retraining and job/task proficiency), we might look for better estimates of the coefficients on these links. Alternatively, if something we thought should have strong effects did not (e.g., attrition), we would examine its links and their coefficients again. This process of refinement can go on until you are satisfied that the model is as refined as you can make it on the basis of the information available or until you feel confident with the results.

Sensitivity Analysis

We have just looked at the major way that the benefits model would be used—to compare two or more approaches. In the preceding example, instead of comparing the use of trainers versus actual equipment, we could have compared three different types of trainers with different capabilities to decide which one was best. In this kind of comparison, the weights and values could be much more precise, since we could use data from functional specifications or actual use for their values.

There is a second way of using the causal model developed: sensitivity analysis. Sensitivity analysis (also called parametric analysis) is a way of identifying the relative importance of any attribute in a training approach. By zeroing or doubling the value of an attribute, and computing all of the derived weights, you can determine the importance of this attribute on the different training outcomes. Alternatively, it is possible to determine the appropriate value of an attribute for a desired level of benefit.

For example, suppose in our example you wanted to know the importance of interactive capabilities on different levels of training outcomes. By setting its weight to 0 and recomputing all of the derived weights for trainers, you could answer this question. The value of the practice outcome would be .60 (.24 + .24 + 0 + .12) for trainers versus .4 for equipment, and the value of job/task proficiency would be .36 for trainers versus .24 for equipment. The value for availability of operational equipment would now be .25 (.14 + .02 + .09) for trainers versus .18 for equipment, and the value of mission readiness would be .16 (.08 + .08) for trainers versus .10 for equipment. In other words, the overall contribution of the interactive capabilities of the trainer to the 8-percent improvement is approximately 2 percent.

Suppose that a four-star general agreed to give you all the money you need for the trainers if you can demonstrate a 10 percent increase in mission readiness as a result of their use (a pretty tall order!). You could use sensitivity analysis to determine what values of outcomes and attribute weights would be required to do this. (You simply work the computations backward). Then the problem becomes finding a company that will make a trainer that meets the specifications you require.

Benefits Analysis: Summing Up

Benefits analysis possesses some desirable features. It allows for partial effects and attenuation of effects, both of which are realistic properties of training systems. No training system, no matter how well organized and staffed, can hope to account for more than some fraction of all of the factors that influence job performance. Similarly, even the very positive outcomes achieved by training are mitigated by other factors.

Benefits analysis also makes it possible to link training system parameters with the goals and objectives of the organization. One of the major problems in the training field is that training developers or managers are unable to convince top executives (or even their bosses) of the need or value of a particular training approach. The benefits model provides a way of linking attributes of the training approach and training outcomes to operational outcomes and goals. For example, mission readiness in our example is actually a high-level military goal. Thus, benefits analysis is a very useful tool in justifying training needs and expenditures.

Finally, benefits analysis provides a way of making subjective judgments or implicit assumptions regarding training effectiveness explicit. The relationship between an attribute of a particular approach and training outcomes is represented by a value that can be disputed and changed. Sure, you may be unhappy having to make subjective estimates for some weights or coefficients. However, you would do this anyway in any kind of cost/benefits analysis. The virture of benefits analysis is that it allows you to make your inferences public and open them to discussion and refinement.

Benefits analysis allows systemization and quantification of what has traditionally been a very *ad hoc* and qualitative procedure. I often get the impression that many training managers think the only way to assess the benefits of a training approach is the way a farmer prices a hog: He looks it over once and drawls, "That there hog's worth fifteen hundred bucks to me."

This is not to say that benefits analysis as outlined in this chapter does not have a long way to go. It is based on two social science methodologies applied to the training domain: econometric modeling and path analysis. Both of these methodologies have considerably more to offer in the refinement of benefits analysis. However, even in its present state, it has proved valuable in assessing training effectiveness and should be a useful tool for you.

You Try It

A large oil company has a significant problem with high accident rates at its oil drilling sites. A problem analysis is conducted and identifies a number of problems underlying the situation: lack of adequate operator training on certain pieces of rig equipment, poor attitudes toward safety, insufficient supervision, poor equipment design, employee fatigue, and lack of necessary physical coordination on the part of some operators. Two of these problems appear to be within the domain of the training department: training on operating procedures and attitudes toward safety.

Further analysis reveals the inadequacies of the present training materials in these two areas. In the case of operating procedures, the employees report that the present workbooks and slide/tape materials do not really convey the complexity of operating the equipment. In addition, it is clear that they lack sufficient practice exercises. Furthermore, the current instruction focuses only on the correct way to do things without showing examples of mistakes and the consequences of mistakes.

As far as attitudes toward safety are concerned, it is apparent that the present workbook and slide/tape materials do not really convey affective information satisfactorily. There is a need to use modeling strategies that portray equipment operators with a positive attitude toward safety (particularly disabled and injured employees). In addition, there is a need to make the safety messages quite specific to the particular job that each different employee does to avoid the "that can't happen in my job" syndrome.

After some pilot studies, it is evident that video is the best instructional medium for the new training. The problem is to decide between delivering it in videotape or videodisc form (both of which are currently in use in the company). Figure 5-6 provides a benefits model for the problem. The attributes being considered are the major ones that differentiate between videotape and videodisc: access time, durability, presentation capabilities, and capacity. The weights are derived as follows. The maximum access time on videodisc averages two seconds; whereas on videotape it is ten seconds (T: .2; D: 1). The durability of videodisc is rated at four years, compared to one year for videotape for the same number of plays (T: .25; D: 1). The videodisc possesses some presentation capabilities which videotape lacks (i.e., slow/fast motion, still frame) and which are considered important for the operator procedures training (T: 0; D: 1). Finally, the capacity of videodisc is at least three times as great as videotape (T: .33; D: 1).

The coefficients shown in Figure 5-6 were developed on the basis of group ratings of the importance of each attribute or outcome on the other outcomes. The group felt that in no case did the identified factors account for more than 80 percent of the variance. In fact, it was felt that the two training factors (i.e., operating procedures and attitudes) only accounted for 40 percent of the total accident rate's variance.

Benefits Analysis

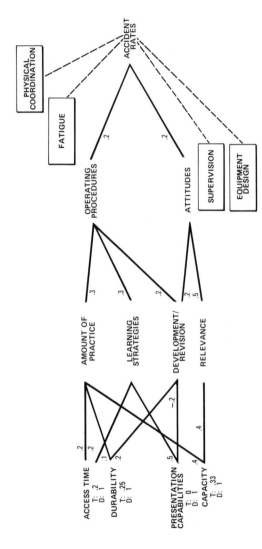

Figure 5-6 Causal Model

78

Following the procedures outlined in Figure 5-7, identify the derived weights for all of the outcomes in the model. How much difference could the use of videotape versus videodisc make in terms of reducing accident rates according to the model? What outcome shows the greatest difference between videotape and videodisc? Which attribute appears to produce the greatest difference between videotape and videodisc?

---

1. Identify all of the attributes, training outcomes and operational outcomes relevant to the problem. Isolate those outcomes which are beyond the scope of training.

2. Identify all of the associations among the attributes and outcomes. Assign coefficients (with values of −1 to +1) to these relations based upon empirical data or expert judgments.

3. Assign relative weights to the different training approaches being compared for each attribute (with values 0 to 1).

4. Compute the desired weights for each outcome using the formula:

$$O_j = \Sigma C_i O_i$$

5. On the basis of the derived weights, draw tentative conclusions regarding relative benefits between training approaches for each outcome.

6. Identify the most critical associations and refine (if possible) the values of the coefficients. Recompute the derived weights and check conclusions.

7. To identify the importance of specific attributes, conduct a sensitivity analysis by setting the value of the weight to zero and computing the derived weights. Compare the difference between these values and those with the originally assigned weight.

Figure 5-7 Procedure for Benefits Analysis

Chapter Six
Measuring Productivity

As you should recall from the introductory chapter, improving efficiency in a training system means achieving the same level of outcomes with fewer resources (i.e., less costs), whereas improving effectiveness amounts to getting better results for the same level of resources. We have now looked at two models that focus on assessing efficiency (i.e., resource requirements and life cycle) and one for gauging effectiveness (i.e., benefits analysis). In this chapter, we will consider productivity analysis, which deals with the combination of effectiveness and efficiency. An increase in training productivity results when better results are obtained for fewer resources.

Productivity Functions

The basis for training productivity models comes from classical economic theory. The most widely accepted production function, attributed to Cobb and Douglas, has the form:

$$O = aL^m C^n$$

where O represents the production output or amount of work accomplished, L represents the amount of labor, C represents the amount of capital, a is a constant, and m and n are exponents for the labor and capital terms. Described in words, this production function states that the amount of work accomplished is the product of the amount of labor and the amount of capital involved. More work (output) can be achieved by increasing the amount of labor or the amount of capital, or both.

In the context of instruction, the output or work to be measured is the amount of learning (i.e., knowledge, skills) that results as a consequence of the instruction. In the educational domain, the measure of instruction is usually student achievement (i.e., grades, competencies) or simply the number of students enrolled and graduated. In the training realm, the measure is typically job proficiency skills, such as improved sales ability, improved service ability, etc. Generally, the "output" that results from training can be related to "work" valued by the organization (e.g., sales volume, number of customers served, number of machines repaired, etc.), as we saw in the previous chapter on benefits analysis.

The labor term of the classical productivity function corresponds to number and quality of the personnel involved in a training system. This includes instructors, managers or administrators, designers or developers, and, of course, training analysts. The capital term represents the facilities, equipment, and materials used in a training system. By increasing either the labor (personnel) or capital (facilities, equipment, and materials) aspects of a training system, the amount of work (training) accomplished should increase.

Figure 6–1 illustrates the nature of productivity functions graphically. If every increase in training resources (i.e., labor and capital) produces the same increment in the amount of training accomplished, line A would describe the productivity function. For example, if doubling the amount of instructors always produced twice as many graduates, line A would be the appropriate function. Curve B represents the case where each increase in training resources produces a smaller increase in training outcomes. Thus, if doubling the number of instructors produces successively fewer increases in the number of graduates, Curve B would be the correct function. Curve C is the opposite case where each increase in training resources results in a larger increase in training outcomes. In our

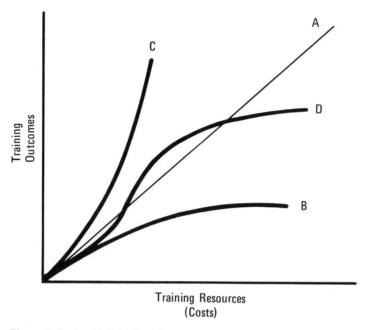

Figure 6-1 Productivity Functions

example, this would mean that for each doubling of instructors, a greater increase in number of graduates would result. Finally, Curve D describes a case where initially the gains are greater than the resource increments but later the resource increments are greater. This would mean that when we first double instructors, we get more than double the number of graduates, but later we get less than double the number.

So far we have looked at the classical form of the productivity function. However, we are quite free to define productivity functions in terms of any variables we want. The following productivity function is a rather important one:

| Training Accomplished | = Trainers × | Training Procedures | × Training Technology |

This can be interpreted as follows. The amount or quality of training accomplished (e.g., as measured by the number of graduates or their job proficiency skills) is a function of the efficiency/effectiveness of the trainers, training procedures, and training technology. This productivity function links training outcomes with the number or skills of the training staff, the nature of the procedures used to design, develop, and deliver the training, and the nature of the training delivery system itself (i.e., classroom-based, mediated self-study, etc.). Furthermore, training procedures and technology are multipliers of the trainer (labor) term. Thus, some level of training can be accomplished with any type or degree of procedures or technology. However, to the extent that the procedures and technology are efficient and/or effective, more or better training will be accomplished. For example, the efficiency/effectiveness of an instructor can be improved through the use of better teaching methods. Similarly, the use of technology (e.g., a computer that scores tests or provides drill and practice exercises) can also improve an instructor's efficiency/effectiveness.

Because technology tends to produce quantum leaps in work potential, it is by far the greater multiplier. If we consider the domain of transportation, it is easy to see how successive technologies—the steam engine (trains, ships), the internal combustion engine (trains, planes, automobiles), and the jet engine (planes, rockets)—have increased our capability to move something from one place to another in a given time unit. In instruction, it is likely that the same kind of productivity increases exist for the technologies of print (books), video (television), and computers (computer-assisted learning), although this has never really been demonstrated in a practical setting.

If we look at productivity from the students' point of view, we can develop a function of the following form:

$$\text{Learning Accomplished} = \text{Student Profile} \times \text{Instructional Presentation} \times \text{Practice}$$

The amount or degree of learning accomplished is a function of the student's profile (i.e., aptitudes, motivation, existing knowledge/skill), the nature of the instructional presentation, and the nature of the practice the student obtains. As with the previous productivity function, the nature of the presentation and the nature of the practice are multipliers on the student's characteristics. Both can only improve the amount of learning accomplished within the range of the student's capabilities and interests. Of the two multipliers, the amount and kind of practice is undoubtedly more important, since it can strongly determine how much learning activity occurs for any given type of presentation.

Productivity functions have some important properties as far as evaluating the cost/benefits of training systems is concerned. The most significant characteristic is that increases in any term of the function increase the amount of training or learning accomplished, but at a diminishing rate. This means that as more money is spent on a particular component, the corresponding gains in terms of skills acquired will decrease. For example, good proficiency in a skill may be achieved by one hour of concentrated practice, but to acquire the skill at an "expert" level may require hundreds of hours of practice, and a "champion" level may require thousands of hours. Another example might be the use of certain media in a training program. A small number of lessons delivered via this media produce significant increases in student performance; however, the use of this media for more lessons produces smaller and smaller effects on performance.

A second important characteristic of the productivity functions is that if *any* term is zero, the output is zero. Thus, if there were no trainers or training procedures or training technology (where technology is broadly defined), there could be no training accomplished. Similarly, without some student profile, presentations, and practice, no learning could be accomplished. The terms included in a productivity function are essential conditions or attributes for instructional outcomes to be achieved in a certain situation.

A third feature of productivity functions is that increasing *all* of the terms by the same factor or percent increases the output to the same degree. This means that if the effectiveness or efficiency of the trainer, training procedures, and training technology are all improved by 10 percent, the overall amount or quality of training will be improved by 10 percent. On the other hand, increasing only one term by 10 percent will produce a much smaller percentage increase on training outcomes. This corresponds to the general observation that in order to bring about a significant overall change in a training system, all major aspects of the system must be improved simultaneously. Improving one thing (e.g., the

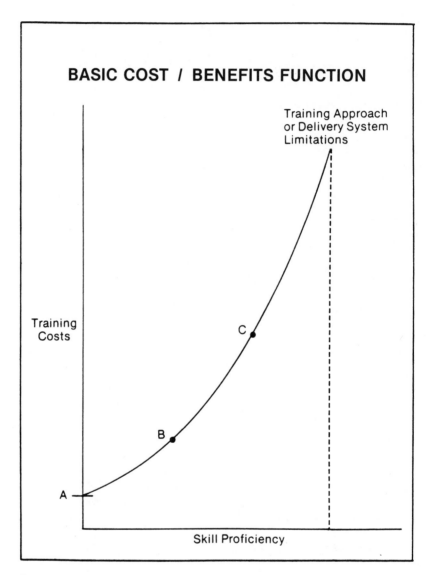

Figure 6-2   Basic Cost/Benefits Function

quality of the training materials) but not changing others (e.g., management of training process, student incentives) may not result in an overall improvement in training. (This relates to the partial causality seen in benefits models.)

How do productivity functions help you assess the cost/benefits of a specific training approach? Suppose that Figure 6-2 represents the actual or predicted relationship between training costs and job proficiency achieved for a particular training situation. Point A represents the baseline costs to produce any training, point B represents a stage of relatively high productivity, and point C represents a diminishing level of productivity. By changing the values of each term in the productivity function relating costs to proficiency, the shape of the curve (and, hence, the productivity) can be changed.

Even though the productivity of a particular approach can be improved, there will always be some point at which that approach reaches its limits in terms of producing increased training outcomes. (Note that this is a practical limitation since the productivity function is not asymptotic.) This means that if points B and C in Figure 6-2 can be identified, it can be determined how much money should be spent upon a particular training approach or delivery system and at what point (i.e., expenditure level) that approach or system should be abandoned in favor of a new one. Figure 6-3 shows how a number of different training approaches or delivery systems might be needed for a complete training program. The first approach would be used to teach one type or level of skill, the second approach for learning of another type or level, and the third approach to teach the final type/level—each maximizing the productivity of that particular approach.

Example: Basic Sales Training

Let's consider an example of how this might work. A major insurance company trains thousands of new agents each year in basic selling skills. There are three major proficiencies that must be acquired:

1. An understanding of the basic concept and principles involved in selling insurance

2. The ability to follow the steps in the basic selling approach

3. The ability to adapt the basic selling approach to different customer needs.

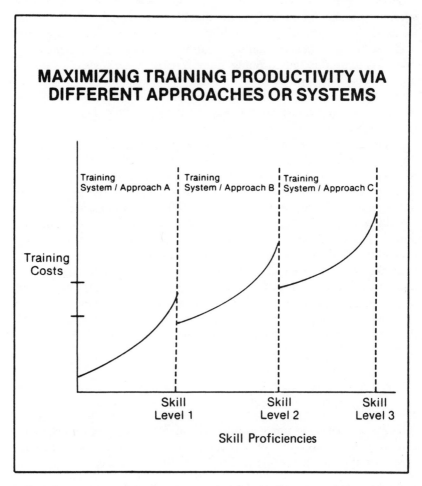

Figure 6-3 Maximizing Training Productivity via Different Approaches or Systems

After trying out many different approaches over the years, the manager of the sales training program has reached the conclusion that no single approach works for all three of these proficiencies. To prove a point, the manager went through student records from different classes in which different approaches had been used, and obtained the data shown in Figure 6–4. These data clearly showed that the classroom/lecture approach was the best for teaching basic concepts and principles, that videotapes with group discussion or role playing between student and instructor were best for learning how to follow the steps in the basic sales approach, and that role playing alone was best for learning how to apply the basic sales approach to a specific customer situation.

On the basis of these data, the manager concluded that to improve the productivity of the basic sales training program, all three approaches would need to be used at different points in the program. The problem

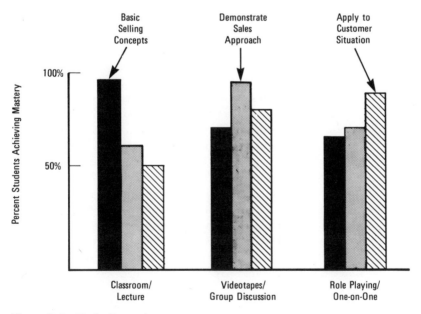

Figure 6-4   Media Comparisons

was to precisely identify these points in terms of the training resources needed and costs involved.

Productivity analysis can be used to do this. The following production function would be suitable:

Selling   = Instructor   × Technology
Proficiency   Preparation   Required

In words, the selling proficiency achieved is a function of the degree of instructor preparation required and the technology required. Both instructor preparation required and the technology required will reflect the approach being used. Thus, the classroom/lecture approach requires different preparation and technology (i.e., equipment, facilities, materials) than does the videotape/group discussion approach, as does the role playing between student and instructor. Both variables can be expressed in dollar values—the costs of the instructor preparation time and the technology involved.

The actual form of the productivity function that would be used would be:

$$SP = A(IP^M) \times (TR)^N$$

where SP is the skill proficiency in appropriate units (e.g., percent achieving mastery), IP represents instructor preparation time expressed in dollars, and TR represents technology required in dollars. A is a constant representing the startup level of a training approach (i.e., how much money must be spent before some minimal level of skill proficiency is achieved). The effect of changing the value of A is to steepen or flatten the productivity curves. The exponents M and N on IP and TR, respectively, determine the shape of the productivity curve. A value between 0 and 1 would result in a decreasing curve (e.g., curve B in Figure 6-1), and a value greater than 1 would produce an increasing curve (e.g., curve C in Figure 6-1). Certain combinations of M and N will produce logistic curves (e.g., curve D in Figure 6-2), which have a point of inflection where an increasing curve becomes a decreasing curve, or vice-versa.

Our training manager is interested in determining values for instructor preparation time and technology required that result in the desired skill proficiency levels on the three different levels of selling skills. To do this, it is necessary to find values of A, M, and N associated with each of the three training approaches. Going back to the data, the expenditures for instructor preparation and technology would be plotted against the student proficiency scores obtained. For these points, a curve (or line) would be fitted, and the values *A*, *M*, and *N* can be determined for the function that most closely generates this curve. Once the values of these parameters have been determined, it is simply a matter of solving the equation for the values of *IP* and *TR* for a given level of *SP*. Thus, our manager would be able to identify the amount of money that could be spent on instructor preparation and technology for a specified level of student proficiency for each approach.

Let's look at a concrete example of this equation. Suppose that the following values for the parameters were obtained from the data:

Approach	A	M	N
Classroom/Lecture	.09	.3	.2
Videotape/Group Discussion	.07	.4	.3
Role Playing/One-on-One	.06	.5	.34

If the desired mastery level was 90 percent, the following equation would be obtained for the role playing approach:

$$90 = (.06)\,(IP)^{.5} \times (TR)^{.34}$$

Solving the equation for *IP* and *TR* gives a set of values such as the following:

IP	TR
10,000	3,375
3,600	15,625
2,500	27,000
1,600	52,734

Thus, to achieve a 90-percent mastery criterion with this approach, it would be necessary to spend $2,500 on instructor preparation (e.g., $2,500 ÷ $100/day = 25 days) and $27,000 on the technology (e.g., videotape equipment, office mockup) or $3,600 on instructor preparation and $15,625 on technology or some other combination.

The manager is now able to make specific decisions about the appropriate levels of expenditures for instructor preparation and technology for the three different approaches for desired levels of student proficiency. The manager is also able to say how much more it would cost in terms of these two variables to achieve a higher level of student proficiency. Alternatively, it is also possible to know what decrease in student proficiency would result if it is necessary to cut the expenditures for these variables. In other words, the manager is able to predict both the effectiveness and efficiency of the sales training program as far as the variables of instructor preparation and technology requirements are concerned.

Return On Investment

Return On Investment (ROI) is the rate of how much something returns relative to how much was invested. Although the concept of ROI can be applied to any of the major models we have discussed, it is most likely to show up in a productivity analysis since we are explicitly looking for improved outcomes with fewer resources. Thus, if you expect to achieve a $100,000 improvement in training results for a $50,000 increase in training costs, our ROI would be $100,000 ÷ $50,000 = 2. Any ROI over 1 means that we are getting out more than we are putting in; any ROI of less than 1 means that we are getting less return than our investment.

Generally, to apply the concept of ROI to cost analyses we must have some quantifiable benefit that can be directly linked up to its costs. However, it is also possible to compute ROI on the basis of cost savings. Thus, if we are using a life cycle model, the investment (R&D, start-up, and transition) costs can be compared to the returns (steady state cost savings). For instance, in the product training example in the previous chapter, the investment consisted of the R&D costs ($150,000), the equipment component of the start-up costs ($22,500 × 3 years = $67,500), and the transition costs ($33,750) for a total of $251,250. The return was the $322,500 saved over the six-year life cycle. Thus, the ROI for the example would be $322,500 ÷ $251,250 = 1.3 in terms of project cost savings over the previous training approach.

ROI is a simple financial indicator of the worth of a particular effort. Because it is not always possible to quantify benefits or outcomes in terms of dollars, ROI may not always be appropriate. In such cases, a benefits analysis is indicated.

Example: Dictation Training

You have recently taken over the position of director of management training for a medium-sized corporation. One day in a conversation with the director of administration, you learn that although all of the secretaries have dictation equipment, it is seldom used by the managers. In fact, only about 20 percent of the current fifty managers use dictation at all. The director of administration points out that dictation is known to increase overall manager productivity by approximately 25 percent in document tasks, and you realize that you should investigate the training aspects of this problem.

Back at your office you calculate the potential benefits of dictation training. From available data, you know that managers spend about a third of their time generating correspondence, reports, proposals, and other documents. Since the annual salary of your managers is approximately $30,000, the annual worth of the time spent generating documents is $10,000. Since dictation could improve this by 25 percent, this would free up 25 percent of their time for other management activities—a value of $2,500 in terms of salary. Since 80 percent (forty) of the managers do not currently use dictation, the total value of their use of dictation would be $2,500 × 40 = $100,000.

You do some "detective" work to find out more about the dictation situation. After talking to a number of different managers and their secretaries, you find out the following:

1. None of the managers has had any dictation training.

2. All of the managers you talked to are interested in improving their document generation productivity.

3. The managers feel that if they had their own portable dictation unit, they would be more likely to dictate than in the current situation of having to share units.

4. The secretaries have a clear preference for dictation over handwritten originals.

On the basis of this information and your cost calculation, you decide to investigate the training programs available. After examining a lot of programs, you identify three that appear promising. The first is a workbook/videotape program, which would take about two hours to complete and costs $750 for forty managers. The second is a half-day seminar, which costs $250 per manager (40 × $250 = $10,000 total). The third is a full-day workshop, which costs $500 per manager (40 × $500 = $20,000 total). By talking to clients who have tried these programs, you find out the following effectiveness data: After one year, the number of participants who are regularly using dictation is 10 percent for the first approach, 50 percent for the second approach, and 75 percent for the third program. The productivity function for these results is shown in Figure 6-5.

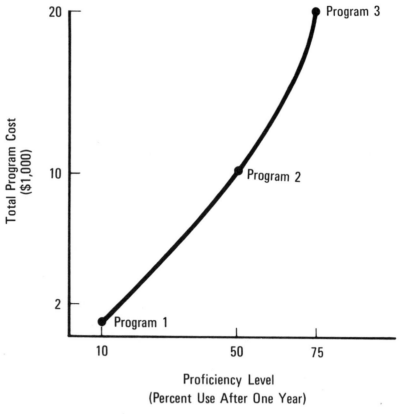

Figure 6-5 Productivity Function for Dictation Training

We can now make some cost comparisons. For each program, we must include the cost of the program, plus the value of the training time (average daily salary of a manager is $100). In addition, we can add the cost of the dictation units (which is not really a training cost) to each of the programs. Thus, the two-hour program costs $750 for the materials, plus $40 \times (\$100 \div 8/2) = \$1,000$ for the training time, plus equipment costs of $40 \times \$100 = \$4,000$, for a total of $5,750. The half-day seminar costs $40 \times \$250 = \$10,000$ for the participants, plus $40 \times (100 \div 8/4) = \$2,000$ for the training time, plus equipment costs of $40 \times \$100 = \$4,000$, for a total of $16,000. The full-day workshop costs $40 \times \$500 = \$20,000$ for the participants, plus $40 \times (\$100 \div 8/8) = \$4,000$ for the training time, plus equipment costs of $40 \times \$100 = \$4,000$, for a total of $28,000.

Using the effectiveness data, we can compute the value of the three programs. The two-hour program results in a 10-percent utilization rate. Since the total value of all forty managers using dictation was $100,000 per year, this program has a dollar value of 10 percent of $100,000 = $10,000. The half-day seminar results in a fifty-percent utilization rate after one year, for a value of $50,000. The full-day workshop with a seventy-five-percent outcome is worth $75,000. On the basis of these calculations, we can compute the ROI of the three programs:

Program	Total Cost	Total Return	ROI
Two hours	$ 5,750	$10,000	1.7
Half day	$16,000	$50,000	3.1
Full day	$28,000	$75,000	2.7

Thus, you conclude that on the basis of ROI, the half-day seminar is the best training approach. (On the other hand, if you had felt that it was more important to have a higher overall utilization of dictation even for a lower ROI, you might have selected the full-day workshop.)

You Try It

Let's suppose that you are the manager of instructional development for a large government agency. One department in your agency is planning the development of a new training program which will involve three

95

media: workbooks, slide/tapes, and computer-based instruction. They are considering a number of possible combinations of these media in each course and they are asking for your input in terms of development costs. You decide to conduct a productivity analysis according to the procedure outlined in Figure 6–6. From past experience, you know that you can predict the development costs fairly well, simply on the basis of the length of the instruction. In other words, the function:

$$\text{Total Development Hours} = A \left(\text{Total Instructional Hours} \right)^N$$

allows you to relate development time to the length of the instruction (where A and N are parameters specific to the media involved). By plotting some data from past development projects, you come up with the following values:

	A	N
Workbooks	10	1.1
Slides/Tapes	60	1.2
Computer-Based Instruction	100	1.5

The values for A indicate that each media has different threshold values to develop, and the values for N indicate that for all three of the media, longer lessons cost proportionately more to develop than shorter lessons, and this difference is greatest with computer-based instruction.

Given these values, and the fact that the average rate of an instructional developer is $10/hour, what are the estimated development costs associated with the following alternative media mixes for a particular course?

	Number of Hours		
	Workbooks	*Slide/Tape*	*CBI*
Alternative 1	10	10	10
Alternative 2	15	10	5
Alternative 3	20	5	5

Suppose that costs of the least expensive alternative must be cut by 20 percent. How many hours of each of these three media would be possible?

96

1. Identify the variables which affect the training outcome you are interested in.

2. Develop a productivity function of the form,

    $$O = AV_1^n \times V_2^m \ldots$$

3. On the basis of data or theoretical considerations, determine the values of all parameters (a, n, m, etc.) for each approach you are comparing.

4. For each approach, determine the values of the particular value(s) of the training outcome you are interested in.

5. Draw conclusions about changes in productivity as a consequence of changes in outcomes and variables.

Figure 6-6 Procedure for Productivity Analysis

Chapter Seven
Data Collection

As you surely realize by now, cost/benefits analysis involves a lot of data collection activity. In fact, it is the data collection activity that often makes the difference between a successful and unsuccessful cost/benefits analysis. Never forget the golden rule of modeling: Garbage In, Garbage Out! No matter how carefully you have defined the problem and constructed your model, if your data are dubious, then your results and conclusions will be too.

The Data Collection Process

To start, let's examine the entire data collection process. Figure 7–1 identifies ten major steps in conducting a cost/benefits analysis, six of which (steps 3 through 8) have to do with data collection. After the appropriate model has been selected and formulated, the data requirements can be identified (step 3). Obviously, the kind of data required will depend on which model you are using. The resource requirements model has the simplest data requirements—the costs of personnel, facilities,

Data Collection

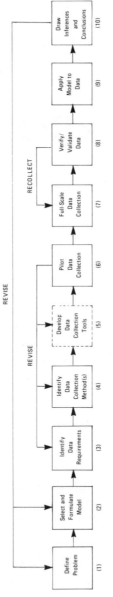

Figure 7-1 Steps in Conducting Cost/Benefits Analysis

equipment, and materials associated with a particular training approach. These kind of data typically come from budgets, accounting records, or other financial sources. Life cycle models have similar data requirements, except that now you are interested in costs that span a number of years and also include R&D, start-up, and transition activities. With a benefits analysis model, you will need very detailed information on training system attributes and outcomes in order to determine values for the weights and coefficients of the causal model. These kind of data are likely to be acquired from expert judgments, empirical results, and outside sources, rather than internal financial records. For productivity models you will primarily need data on resource costs relative to outcomes achieved (i.e., how much did it cost to produce certain results). Since normally the cost data and outcome data (e.g., test scores, job performance measures) will be collected separately, you will need to rely on expert judgments or empirical findings to link them up.

For any of the models, data will be needed in order to check your assumptions regarding benefits. In the example in Chapter Four, one of the assumptions made in switching from "canned" videotaped training to "live" video conferencing was that this switch would not adversely affect sales or service performance. To check this important assumption, sales/service performance data were collected during a pilot study. In the example in Chapter Five, cost savings were calculated on the basis of recovering lost sales due to reduced training time. In order to estimate the value of these sales, data were required on the average sales volume/day of the trainees. In the example in Chapter Six, the manager assumed that different approaches achieved different levels of proficiencies, and obtained data to support this assumption. Every time assumptions are made regarding effectiveness or cost savings, data will be needed to back up these assumptions.

Once the model has been formulated, it is usual to make up "dummy" data to test out the model. This should be done as part of the data requirements identification step since it will likely reveal some important characteristics of the data to be collected, such as the amount and precision needed. Normally, there is a certain minimum amount of data required to get acceptable results as well as a point beyond which more data does not help. Similarly, there is a range of acceptable precision for the data. Data that fall outside of this range (either because it is too crude

101

or too precise) is not useful and will be a waste of time to collect. Note that the precision of the data required will depend very much on the nature of analysis. In some cases, data to two decimal places is appropriate; in other situations, data that are within a tolerance of plus or minus 10 percent is acceptable. It all depends on what kind of data are available, the precision of the model, and the importance of the decision being made. In general, you start off with relatively low precision specifications and tighten these up as the model and data collection activity is refined (see steps 6 and 8). You should be careful not to set unrealistic requirements for the amount or precision of the data needed at the beginning of the data collection activity—you may not get any further! On the other hand, if you realize at this step that the amount or precision of the data required is clearly not feasible, then this is a good time to stop and rethink the model.

Having identified the data required, we can move on to the next step—identifying the appropriate data collection method(s). There are basically five methods: questionnaires, interviews, experiments, analysis, and observation. Questionnaires are a very common way of collecting cost/benefits data probably because they are usually the least expensive method. For example, if a resource requirements or life cycle model is being developed, a questionnaire can be sent to different training managers to have them provide estimates of the personnel, facility, equipment, and materials requirements associated with the training programs they manage or administer. With benefits or productivity analysis, questionnaires could be used to obtain judgments of the relationships between training system attributes and outcomes or between training costs and outcomes.

Interviews are a second common way of obtaining cost/benefits data. They can be either face-to-face or via telephone, and individual or group. They may also be structured (following some sort of prespecified format or questions) or informal. In general, interviews are used instead of questionnaires when different data are required from different people, when the data are considered too sensitive to be provided in written form, or when the data are required very quickly. Clearly, data obtained via interviews costs more to collect than questionnaire data. They also may be more reliable since the data collector may be able to assess the validity of the source on the basis of documentation provided or the sincerity of the interviewee (see step 8).

Obtaining cost/benefits data via experiments is not very common in the training field, although the military and a few organizations do have traditions of experimentally assessing the cost/benefits of different training approaches through R&D studies. Needless to say, this is a relatively expensive (and lengthy) way of obtaining cost/benefits data, since experiments must be designed, run, and analyzed. However, it is also the best and, in many cases, the only way of obtaining certain cost/benefits information. This is typically the case with assumptions about the relative effectiveness of one approach over another. While the available research literature may indicate that approach A is as good as approach B, in general, you may need to convince yourself or your boss that this will be true in your training system. Thus, you may need to conduct an experiment to show that both approaches result in equal levels of sales performance, customer service, unit production, mission readiness, or whatever the important performance outcome is. If you are doing a benefits or productivity analysis, you will be interested in finding out how much better one approach is in terms of certain operational outcomes or job performance.

You may be able to collect the data you need by analyzing other sources of information. These sources may be research journals, conference presentations, government reports, or your own organization's financial records. Many times it is much faster and less difficult to seek out the data you require from existing documentation rather than try to get it from the original source via questionnaires and interviews or conduct costly experiments. For example, cost information on resources utilized in a number of training programs may be obtained by interviewing the managers of these programs. However, it may be quicker and easier to obtain this data from the accounting or data processing department that keeps detailed records of all resource utilization (i.e., hours worked, equipment operating and maintenance costs, materials bought or sold, etc.). While it may take some "detective" work to find the numbers you are looking for, they may turn out to be more accurate than the ones obtained from the original sources and be a lot easier to get. (See the discussion in the next section on data collection problems.)

Finally, necessary data may be collected by simply observing. In many cases, no one will know the answer to a particular question you are asking because it has never been asked before. Even simple statistics, such as the average and range of completion time for a certain training program or the average utilization level of training facilities or equipment, may not be known. On the other hand, the data needed may be much more sophisticated, such as what are the real benefits of a certain training approach or what factors really affect a certain training outcome. To obtain such data it may be necessary to have someone observe and record the parameters of interest in actual training situations. Like experimentation, observation is frequently one of the best ways of collecting valid data. It is also one of the most time-consuming and expensive.

It should be understood that none of these five methods of data collection is exclusive and you are likely to use a combination of them in any cost/benefits analysis. For example, general information that is the same across many groups could be obtained via questionnaires with unique information obtained through telephone or face-to-face interviews. Information required for the comparison of two different approaches or to support cost saving assumptions might be obtained via analysis or experiments. Finally, observation and analysis might be used to verify and validate data (see step 8) collected via questionnaires and interviews.

One of the possible consequences of having identified the appropriate data collection method(s) is that you may need to develop some data collection tools or instruments (step 5). These would include questionnaires, structured interview guides, experimental procedures and apparatus, observation (behavior) recording forms, and library or information service search requests. This step will not always be necessary since many interviews, observations, or analyses may be made without any prior preparation. On the other hand, for the purpose of standardizing and documenting your data analysis methods, it is a good idea to at least use some sort of form for any kind of data collection activity (even if only a phone log or activity memo).

Now you are ready to collect data. However, before leaping in head first, it is extremely valuable to begin with a pilot data collection (step 6). The purpose of a pilot data collection step is to try out your data collection methods and determine whether the data obtained matches the requirements of the model. The pilot data collection should include all of the sources and types of data you eventually plan to collect; however, it should be limited to a very small amount of data. If your actual data collection effort will be quite large, you may wish to randomly select or sample some sources and types. For example, suppose you plan on collecting data from one hundred locations within your organization and you run your pilot data collection only at your own site. There may be some significant problems collecting data at the other sites, which you wouldn't discover until the full scale data collection was underway. In this case, you would want to ensure that your pilot data collection includes four or five other sites.

There are three possible outcomes of your pilot data collection step. The first is that you get exactly the data you expected with no unanticipated difficulties. This is highly unlikely. The second possible outcome, also unlikely, is that you abandon the particular cost/benefits model you were trying or the whole idea of a cost/benefits analysis. In general, having gotten as far as a pilot data collection, you have the right idea—although you may have picked the wrong model. The third outcome, and the most usual, is that the data are not quite what you expected or are more difficult to collect than you had anticipated. Under these circumstances, you would check to see if the data requirements of your model need to be changed or if you need to revise your data collection methods or tools. The possible problems are numerous: the data are not precise enough; the data are incomplete, out of date, or not available; the data are expressed in different terms or units than desired; the data take too long or are too expensive to obtain; or insufficient data were collected (see discussion in the next section).

As a consequence of the pilot data collection step, you should have refined your data collection requirements, methods, and tools. (Note that the purpose of the pilot is not to collect useful data, but to simply check everything out.) Now you are ready to proceed with full-scale data collection (step 7). At this point, it is a matter of seeing that all of the necessary data are collected. If the amount of data are relatively large, it is likely that the data would be entered into a computer database for subsequent analysis.

After the data are collected (or while data collection is still underway), it is necessary to verify or validate the data (step 8).[1] This involves check-

---

[1]Anyone with an accounting background will recognize this step as the process of auditing. In fact, any auditor will be able to provide dozens of useful techniques for data verification and validation.

ing the accuracy and correctness of the data obtained. There are two goals in this step: to determine how good or bad your data are (i.e., how closely they match reality) and to replace data that are unsatisfactory. This step is critical; it avoids the "Garbage In, Garbage Out" problem and allows you to defend and believe the results of your cost/benefits analysis.

There is basically only one way to properly verify and validate your data: independent corroboration. You must try to find two or more independent sources for each data item you collect. For example, if the data item is the average number of course hours per student, you could collect this from training managers via a question on a questionnaire, interview students or instructors, observe some actual courses, or check accounting records to see how much time the average student or instructor indicates on salary timesheets. Now, you are likely to get somewhat different numbers from each of these sources, and this is a measure of the possible accuracy of this item. If the data you have obtained deviate significantly (e.g., 50 percent or more) from the other measures of this item, then you have reason to go back to your source and find out why the data obtained deviate. It is likely that the data request was misinterpreted, the wrong number provided, or the data simply fabricated. Sometimes you may discover that all measures of the "same" data item produce different results. This may be due to different definitions of what costs the item refers to, redundant costs, or different biases on the part of the sources. In this circumstance, you must define your data requirement more exactly, so that the alternative interpretations can be eliminated. However, having done this you must go back to your sources and recollect that data item since they may provide different data with the new definitions.

A second way to obtain corroboration of your data is to derive some result from the data and check this. For example, if you have costs on all of the components of a certain training program, you should be able to check their sum against another estimate of the total cost of that program obtained from a budget or financial report. Similarly, the average number of student hours for a course multiplied by the total number of students in that course should result in the total student hours associated with the course. This should correspond to estimates of instructor time, equipment, facilities, and materials used for the course. Thus, if 4,000 student hours are calculated for a course, but 6,000 hours of equipment use or faculty time were also associated with that course, some further investigation would be in order.

Clearly, it is not possible nor necessary to check every single data item.[2] It is sufficient to sample each source and type of data to ensure that there were no obvious deviations in the data collection process. Normally, one would only further check exceptions, i.e., data resulting in a computation that is considerably out of range. After working with the model and data thus far, you will have developed certain expectations about how things should come out. You will easily notice any results that differ from these expectations. Unfortunately, you will be less likely to catch errors that result in the data coming out the way you expected.

Once the data have been verified to the extent possible or desired, you are ready to do some modeling (step 9). Once the model has been applied to data, certain inferences and conclusions can be drawn (step 10). Usually these conclusions will be in terms of the cost/benefits of one training approach versus another. However, sometimes the conclusions are that a different model is required to address the original problem or that the original problem as defined was not the real problem. These apparent "failures" are not really as worthless as they might seem. One of the most important outcomes of a cost/benefits analysis is an improved understanding of a particular training system or approach. As a consequence of this better understanding, you may realize that your initial conceptualization of the problem was wrong or that you selected the wrong model. This is a step forward. Now you must redefine the problem and try another model. With a little luck, some of the data you have collected will also be useful in your next analysis.

There is often a developmental sequence associated with the four types of models discussed in the preceding chapters, which is largely determined by the availability of data. The kinds of cost/benefits questions asked initially tend to be rather general and focus on comparing approach A versus approach B at a given time, i.e., the resource requirements model. The kind of data required by this model can usually be ob-

---

[2]On the other hand, if the data are in a computer database, it is relatively simple to write a range-checking program which checks the size of numbers or identifies any that are significantly different from the rest. This can be done while the data are being entered or before they are used in a model.

tained via questionnaires, interviews, and analysis of budgets or other readily available financial documents.

Next, interest is generated in being able to compare the cost/benefits for an entire life span, i.e., life cycle cost models. This entails data on R&D, start-up, and steady state costs, making an historical data base necessary. To the extent that resource requirements cost analyses have been conducted in the past, these data will be available. Otherwise, they will have to be estimated from past records and sometimes memory.

Resource requirement and life cycle cost models often stimulate an interest in a more detailed look at the underlying relationships between costs and benefits as provided by benefits or productivity analysis. Both of these types of models have quite sophisticated data requirements, and it is generally easier to collect if cost-tracking procedures are already in use. On the other hand, even existing cost-tracking procedures may be inadequate for the kind of data needed in these models.

The practical consequences of the different data requirements of the four models are that it will normally take you longer and cost more to collect the data needed for benefits and productivity models than the resource requirements or life cycle models. The resource requirements model usually has the simplest data collection requirements. Thus, it is often a good idea to start with this model in order to establish some data collection traditions in your organization before moving up to a more demanding model. On the other hand, if the problem clearly calls for a benefits or productivity analysis, then you should go ahead with these models. But be prepared for a tough time collecting data!

Data Collection Problems

In case you do not already know it, data collection is almost always a tedious and frustrating business! It requires a lot of patience and persistence. (If you lack these qualities, better find someone who has them to collect data for you.) In general, you will find people reluctant to provide the data you want. Some typical excuses are:

"This information is so out of date and rough that it wouldn't be of any use to you."

"That data doesn't exist."

"I don't have that data . . . try Shopenmeyer."

"I can't get that for you until _____."

"I'm not authorized to give you that data."

This reluctance is based upon the following kinds of fears:

1. The data will be somehow used against them.

2. The data will be used inappropriately.

3. The data collection will take too much of their time.

4. The data collection is a waste of time.

You should realize that these are all potentially legitimate fears. For example, cost data are often collected in order to justify a reduction in resources (e.g., instructors, facilities). This could translate into a budget cut for a particular training program or department. This is not something that managers who are affected by that reduction are going to see very positively even if it results in improved efficiency for the rest of the organization. The second fear arises from the feeling that the data provided will be misunderstood and, hence, used incorrectly (possibly leading to fear number 1). For example, a manager may provide data on the number of instructors associated with a particular program. It may turn out that these instructors have other duties and only spend about half of their time on that particular program, but because the questionnaire did not ask about this, it is "hidden" information. This could easily lead to a misunderstanding of why such a relatively large number of instructors are associated with that course. There are always many such cases of "hidden" information in data provided.

The third fear is often created through past experiences with data collection activities. Those who collect data often fail to realize that while it may only take them a few hours to develop a questionnaire or interview requesting ten data items, it could take a respondent two days or two weeks to gather the data requested. Remember that your data collection activity is an imposition on one's regular duties (which one's job performance is evaluated upon). Great care must be taken to ensure that you collect only the data that is absolutely essential, and that your data collection methods and tools are designed to minimize the time required by the respondents.

The fourth fear is also often created by past experiences with data collection activities. People in operating and field positions often view "studies" as some kind of "make work" project with little real importance. It is very common for respondents to take considerable time providing data and then never find out what happened to the data or how it was used. Under these circumstances, you can see why they have no interest in taking any time to provide data for your study.

It is up to you to counter these fears as part of your data collection activity. The simplest way of doing this is with a preparatory letter or memo that goes to all those who will be providing data. In this letter you should:

1. State a rationale for why the data are being collected and a clear description of what will be done with a data. It is essential that you find a way of explaining the end result of the cost/benefits analysis so that it has some perceived value to those providing the data.

2. Give a description of what feedback they will receive as a consequence of providing data (e.g., a report, a decision) and when to expect this. It is critical that some kind of feedback be provided even if only a memo outlining the results of the analysis.

3. Provide a deadline indicating the date by which the data must be provided.

4. Describe the steps being taken to ensure the confidentiality of the data provided.

5. Name a person to contact (i.e., name and phone number) to talk to regarding problems in collecting the data.

6. Provide a signature by the highest ranking member of the organization you can get to sign.

Figure 7-2 provides an example of such a letter. While a letter of this sort will not eliminate all of the fears discussed, it will help. You can still expect, however, to make follow-up calls on many of the sources to personally allay their concerns. You can also anticipate not being successful with everyone!

110

TO: Mr. A.B. Shopenmeyer
Manager, Maintenance Training

RE: Cost Benefits Study

As you probably know, Corporate E&T is studying the cost benefits of developing more self-study training programs which can be used directly in the field. We have found that the existing self-study programs allow us to improve the effectiveness and efficiency of our training activities.

In order to conduct the study, we need you to complete the attached questionnaire and return it to us by July 15. In addition, it is possible that you will be receiving a follow-up phone call to verify your data.

The information from this study will be used to reach a decision regarding the development of further self-study training programs in the organization. A meeting to which you will be asked to attend will be scheduled for the end of August.

The data you provide will be treated as company confidential. We ask you to identify yourself on the questionnaire in case follow-up is needed. Once the data collection is completed, these forms and the identity of the original sources will be destroyed.

If you have any questions regarding the study or the questionnaire, please feel free to contact John Appleyard at extension 3045.

Thank you for your cooperation.

J.B. Rhinegold
VP, Operations

ds/JBR

Figure 7-2   Sample Memo

This brings us to problems that will arise once you have finished your initial data collection and begin to look at your data. The major problem will be that you have a lot of missing items. As a general rule, people are able to provide most, but not all, of what you wanted. Furthermore, people will often provide a combined value for several items that they normally lump together but that you wanted individually. For these

111

problems associated with partial data, you have three alternatives. You can go back to the sources and ask them to provide what you originally requested. Alternatively (or if this fails), you can estimate the value using an average computed from the other data. Or, you can simply do your analysis with partial data, adjusting your computations accordingly.

Probably the most important thing you should remember about the data collection activity is that it is a repeating cycle rather than a one-shot effort. You will need to go back for additional data many times, possibly using different data collection methods and tools each time. Even after you have begun to model, you will still need to refine or recollect data. In fact, it is likely that you will need to continue collecting data even after you think you have reached your conclusions. There is usually someone in the final decision-making meeting who asks about something you do not have data on, but should have.

Chapter Eight
Planning and Forecasting

In the preceding chapters, we have been concerned with the details of the different models and data collection. This chapter looks at cost/benefits analysis in the broader context—as a tool for planning and forecasting. One of the important things discussed in this chapter is the limitations associated with cost/benefits analysis.

Dealing with Uncertainty

One of the major job functions of a manager or administrator is to plan. Planning activity manifests itself in the form of budgets, project schedules, performance objectives, operating plans, etc. All of these planning activities have one thing in common: they involve dealing with uncertainty. The task of a manager is to reduce uncertainty as much as possible (thereby guaranteeing certain outcomes such as improved sales or profits).

Forecasting is the name given to the specific activity of trying to predict some future outcome. There are a large number of formal methodologies and techniques used in forecasting, including trend analysis (i.e., time series), regression analysis, polling, delphi, and simulation modeling. In general, forecasting and planning go hand in hand, although in practice only a relatively small number of managers actually use formal forecasting methods on a regular basis.

The planning responsibilities of training managers and administrators focus on the following kinds of forecasts:

1. Predicting the resources (i.e., personnel, facilities, equipment, and materials) needed for current and future training programs,

2. Predicting how many trainees will be needed, where, and when,

3. Predicting what kind of job skills will be needed and what kind of background will be desirable.

Let's consider each of these in the context of the four types of models we have studied.

Resources

The first requirement is addressed by the resource requirements and life cycle models. Using these models, the resources associated with a given approach or program can be projected, either for an immediate period (i.e., next year) or long term. However, the benefits and productivity analysis models may also be used to forecast resources needed. Benefit analysis can provide a detailed projection of specific training parameters needed to achieve a certain training or operational outcome. These training parameters translate into particular resources required. Similarly, productivity analysis can identify what level of resources are required for certain outcomes in terms of skill levels or job performance. As was discussed in Chapter Six, a large training program might require a combination of different approaches. Productivity analysis can be used to determine the optimal development or delivery costs associated with each approach.

Example: New Product Training

Suppose that you are the director of training for a major aircraft manufacturer that has just decided to go ahead with production of a new jetliner. (Note the product could just as well be computers, trucks, weapons systems, etc.) It is your responsibility to plan the various training programs associated with the plane. This includes the training of all the manufacturing personnel who will fabricate and assemble the planes, the technicians who will service the planes once they begin to fly, as well as the initial cadre of aircrew who fly the plane (pilots, attendants, baggage handlers, etc.). Based upon training data from past aircraft, as well as input from engineers, human factors specialists, and your own training analysis, you develop a set of resource requirement models to represent the projected steady state costs for each different training program. You then develop a life cycle cost model that tracks all of the different programs across the different stages (i.e., R&D studies, startup, transition, steady state). One of your biggest headaches is to identify the best transition plan for the instructors, facilities, equipment, and materials from existing training programs for other aircraft to the new program. You must determine when each program should start and the training throughput for each month based upon the projected production and delivery of the aircraft and the total training resources available.

There are many other questions you must investigate. For each program, there are a large number of possible approaches and methods. You develop benefits and productivity models keyed to the training outcomes and job performance skills postulated. (Since none of these jobs actually exist yet, you have to make inferences based upon existing jobs and task analyses). The benefits analysis models provide you with the fine-grained information needed to select among particular training approaches and methods, while the productivity analysis provides you with more general information on the optimal sequence of approaches and methods to use as well as cost projections. The productivity analysis also provides cost estimates for development of the training programs and materials.

After about three months of formulating models, collecting data, and applying the models to the data, you have reached a tentative set of conclusions about the approaches you intend to follow in each program and the estimated resources needed to design, develop, implement, and evaluate these approaches. Alas, a few days before you are scheduled to turn in your numbers, you are informed that due to heavy initial demand for the plane, the first year's production will be approximately doubled. Now, you must spend the next two days and nights rerunning all of your models and data (fortunately they are in the form of computer programs and data bases) to come up with new figures. While this is not much fun, one of the great virtues of systematic planning methodology is that it takes you very little time to investigate variations or changes in the variables once you have developed the models.

Number of Trainees

The second type of forecasts have to do with the number of trainees needed, where they will be needed and when, and are primarily a function of the operational needs of the organization. Thus, the number of sales or services representatives needed, the number of bus drivers or pilots, or the number of soldiers or tank gunners is determined by the particular dynamics (e.g., new products, company growth, changes in market demands, wars) of the organization and its mission. Generally, the nature of long-term needs are known in advance (e.g., new products planned, new increases in transportation needs, new weapons systems procured) and this allows training projections to be made. On the other hand, the future always brings surprises (e.g., planned products are cancelled, gasoline shortages or mass firings, wars) that often produce relatively sudden training demands.

For these types of forecasts, life cycle and benefits analysis models are likely to be most useful. Life cycle models allow systematic exploration of different benefits of startup, transition, and steady-state periods with different numbers or locations of students associated with these periods. Each different combination of time, place, and student volume represents a different situation to be compared (even though the actual training methods or approach may be the same). Benefits analysis models would be used similarly, except that with the benefits model it would be possible to look at many more factors that affect the outcome of interest. For example, the number of new trainees needed is affected not only by operational needs (such as new products or weapons) but also by attrition during training and employee turnover. The benefits model allows all of these factors to be taken into account.

Example: Teller Training

In this example, your plight is to be training director of a large nationwide bank. Your current preoccupation is teller training. The problem is that the bank is about to embark on an ambitious expansion program that will result in the opening of twenty-four new branches in five states during the next three years. You must develop a plan to train all of the new tellers that will be required for these new branches.

The problem has a number of different facets (most real world problems do). The basic problem is to determine how many tellers to train in what locations and when. In addition, a new on-line banking system will be installed in the new branches, and you have never trained tellers on this type of equipment before. Furthermore, the new branches will feature drive-up windows and automatic cash dispensers. As a final twist, to comply with a new equal rights amendment of the Fair Practices Hiring Act, you must hire approximately an equal number of male and female tellers. However, in the past, virtually all of the tellers have been female and you must now modify your training programs, facilities, and equipment to accommodate this change as well.

After realizing that it is too early for you to retire and ascertaining that there is absolutely nobody else you can dump this problem on, you start work on a life cycle model comparing some of the different possible approaches. One of the major factors to be examined is the location of the training: Should it be all done at a central training center or should it be done locally at each branch? A second consideration is the question of cross-training: Should all tellers be taught how to work the drive-up windows and automatic cash dispensers? A third question is whether the built-in training for the on-line banking system will be sufficient (as the computer company claims) or whether you will need to supplement this. Furthermore, the thought crosses your mind that you might be able to do a large amount of the training via the system since each teller has access to his or her own terminal.

To get some answers on these questions, you develop a benefits analysis that allows you to compare different training approaches (i.e., centralized versus local, separate versus job cross-training, classroom versus computer) on all of the outcomes relating to satisfactory teller job performance. In addition, the benefits model lets you examine the possible advantages and disadvantages of coed training in terms of variables such as motivation, attrition, competition, and achievement. On the basis of the conclusions you draw from the benefits analysis, you are able to formulate four different approaches to investigate with the life cycle model. After looking at different startup, transition, and steady state periods, you reach some conclusions about the best approach and the estimated costs associated with it.

While the board accepts your recommendations regarding the best approach, they insist that you find a way to do it for substantially less money. Back you go to your models, and a week later you present a series of options to the board, each with different cost and reduced levels of effectiveness. The board accepts your lowest cost alternative and directs you to produce the effectiveness levels associated with the original proposal. You accept your fate, knowing that retirement is only a few years away.

Skills

The third kind of forecast, skill levels and trainee backgrounds, is best suited to benefits and productivity analysis models. Benefits analysis models can be used to determine the way in which different kinds of skills (represented as training outcomes) affect operational outcomes. For example, in the sales training example in Chapter Five, three categories of job skills (product knowledge, selling techniques, interpersonal skills) affected the operational outcome of interest (increased sales). A new product may not only require new product knowledge but also different selling techniques and interpersonal skills.[1] Productivity analysis permits direct examination of the relationship between student backgrounds or ability levels and skill proficiencies achieved through training. Thus, the question is, for a given type of training, what type of aptitudes or skills are desirable?

Example: Robots on the Assembly Line

This time you are the training director of a large heavy equipment manufacturing company. Your company recently completed a pilot study with a robot assembly line and was very impressed with the results. They have developed a modernization plan that will involve the gradual conversion of the company's six major plants to completely robotized assembly lines, and you have been asked to formulate a training plan to accommodate this. As part of a union agreement, the company is obligated to retrain its own employees to operate, program, and maintain the robots rather than hire people from outside. Since considerably fewer assembly line employees will be needed once the robots are installed, employees have the choice of being retrained, retiring early, or (eventually) being laid off.

The problem you face as training director is to determine what kinds of retraining options are possible, given certain existing levels of ability and skill, and what the retraining programs will involve. After spending some time conducting task analyses and developing job models of existing robot assembly lines at other companies similar to the ones expected at your own company, you have a reasonable idea of what job skills and abilities you will have to retrain. You then develop a series of productivity models based upon existing types and levels of skills of employees and the types and levels of skills needed. By running these models, you are

---

[1] The switch from selling typewriters to word processing systems, which occurred in the early 1980s, is a good case in point. Not only was the product knowledge much more complex, but the sales techniques changed (from selling individual products to systems) and the customers changed (from office supervisors to middle/senior managers), requiring different interpersonal skills.

able to draw some conclusions about which retraining paths are most cost effective and which ones are prohibitively expensive and unlikely to succeed. On the basis of this information, you make recommendations to senior management, outlining what types of job retraining paths seem best and what the estimated costs of this retraining will be. You add the caveat that while you have recommended the optimal retraining paths, no employee should be prevented from retraining for any new job he or she is interested in. You also point out, however, that each deviation from the optimal path will likely cost the company more in terms of training time and costs.

Planning for Different Training Needs

So far in this chapter, we have looked at three forecasting situations that are common in the training domain, and discussed how different models relate to these three situations. There is another way of discussing planning and forecasting considerations—according to different types of training.

Throughout this book, we have basically treated all types of training alike. As far as the mechanics of how the models work, the data required, and how they are applied to the data, it really makes little difference what kind of training is involved. However, when it comes to the use of the models for planning purposes, there are some differences worth discussing.

Figure 8-1 lists ten major types of training. As will become clear, a particular training application might fit into more than one of these categories (i.e., they are not exclusive). Furthermore, this is not an exhaustive list—there are other kinds of training not covered by the ten categories (although special purpose takes care of most other types).

Operator training is an extremely broad category of training, covering any instruction in which a person is taught how to use a piece of equipment, machine, or device. It includes bus drivers and pilots, computer operators, machine operators (i.e., assembly lines or factories), bulldozer operators, radar operators and, of course, telephone operators. By

1. Operator

2. Maintenance (Service)

3. Administrative/Clerical

4. Sales

5. Management

6. Customer (Consumer)

7. Vocational (Trades)

8. Emergency Services

9. Safety

10. Special Purpose

Figure 8-1 Major Types of Training

and large, the nature of such training involves the learning and practice of procedures associated with certain equipment.

Almost everything that is operated must also be maintained or serviced. Thus, maintenance technicians must be trained to repair buses and aircraft, computers, assembly line machines, bulldozers, radar, and telephones. In addition, there is a need to repair consumer devices such as appliances, photocopiers, automobiles, watches, and stereos. Maintenance training normally involves learning how equipment operates and the acquisition of problem-solving skills (i.e., troubleshooting). One of the distinctive problems of maintenance training is that it is seldom possible to train someone for all the different types of equipment or faults that they will have to repair—generalization is always necessary.

Administrative or clerical training involves the teaching of procedures associated with customer billing, inventory, bookkeeping, personnel records, etc. Word processing training could belong here although it may also be considered operator training. Unlike the procedures associated with operator training, administrative procedures involve cognitive learning (mostly memory) rather than psychomotor. Another feature of administrative training is that it is often unique to an organization, i.e., an individual must learn the particular procedures for bookkeeping or billing for that organization.

Sales training could include the training of sales clerks (retail), sales representatives (equipment or products), or sales agents (insurance or services). Regardless of the type of sales involved, certain selling techniques and interpersonal skills are essential.

Management training spans supervision through middle management to senior executive level. It focuses primarily on interpersonal skills (i.e., communication, negotiation) but also involves the teaching of many specific techniques (budgeting, project management, leadership, etc.). One of the important aspects of both sales and management training is that a great deal of its success depends on the aptitudes and personality of the individual.

Customer or consumer training is actually a special case of operator training in which individuals usually teach themselves how to use a product or service. This is true for almost all devices found in a home (e.g., appliances, lawnmowers, telephones, stereos, etc.). Such self-training comes from manuals supplied with the product or books purchased by the customer. Note that for most business products (e.g., copiers, word processors, paging systems) some type of training is provided by the vendor. In a few special instances, consumer training is provided or certified by the government (e.g., automobiles, shortwave radio).

Vocational training involves the acquisition of specialized skills or trades (e.g., plumbers, electricians, surveyors, carpenters, masons, etc.). Vocational training is often done via state or privately run schools and usually involves some sort of apprenticeship. Unlike the other types of training discussed, vocational training normally takes place over an extended period (i.e., months or years).

Emergency services training encompasses law enforcement, firefighting, hospital and ambulance staff, and miscellaneous others (e.g., ski patrol, first aid, etc.). This type of training does not resemble any of the other types discussed because of the stressful nature of the work situations and the special tools or techniques involved.

Safety training is a special class of operator or maintenance training that involves teaching people certain procedures to follow and avoid. Safety training receives special consideration because of the dangerous consequences associated with the failure to do things right in certain situations. There are various operations (such as oil drilling, mining, nuclear power plants, public transport, weapons systems) in which safety training is paramount.

Finally, there are many types of special purpose training programs that involve unique skills or knowledge. Examples include air traffic controllers, bartenders, travel agents, accident investigators, brokers, intelligence agents, loan officers, hotel management, and many kinds of military jobs. Special purpose training can be obtained through formal courses, on-the-job apprenticeships, or simply self-training.

How do the four different models relate to the type of planning associated with these ten types of training? The resource requirements model applies when one or more approaches are to be compared for a given period. This is a type of planning activity that could be carried on in any of the ten training areas. It is particularly useful in those domains where training programs and curriculum changes on a continuous but irregular basis and short-term comparisons need to be made.

This would be true of administrative/clerical training in which procedures are frequently revised (e.g., consider government agencies and regulatory legislation), and also in sales training as new selling strategies are devised.

Life cycle models are especially useful for training programs that are based on equipment or products. This would include most types of operator and maintenance training, as well as sales, customer, emergency services, safety, and special purpose training, to the extent that they are based on equipment. Any type of administrative training involving the use of some form of computer system (e.g., word processing, online billing) would also be included. As long as the equipment remains in service (or the product is sold), there will be a need for operator and maintenance training. During this life cycle, there are likely to be a number of different training approaches used and, hence, a need for life cycle analysis. For large, complex pieces of equipment (e.g., planes, submarines, computer systems, microwave relay stations, assembly lines), the training is likely to involve several different stages (i.e., classroom, simulations, on-the-job), and life cycle analysis is useful for planning this too. On the other hand, life cycle cost models are not likely to be helpful in situations where training is relatively changeable, such as sales (retail or service), management, administrative/clerical (nonequipment), and customer (service).

Benefits analysis is useful in identifying ways to improve effectiveness in a training program or system. Clearly, its major application lies in those areas where a premium is placed on satisfactory job performance. This would include operation and maintenance of expensive or potentially dangerous equipment (e.g., aircraft, public transport, weapons systems), any type of safety training, and special purpose training such as air traffic control. It would also include areas such as sales, management, and emergency services where inadequate job performance is likely to have significant consequences (lost sales, failed businesses, lost lives).

Actually, productivity analysis is more likely to be used than benefits analysis to assess effectiveness in people-based training areas such as sales, management, and emergency services. This is because many of the job performances in these areas are relatively intangible and are better measured macroscopically. Thus, rather than try to measure the relationship between the selling skills of sales representatives and their individual sales performance, it is easier to study functions relating parameters of sales training (e.g., duration, end-of-course scores) to subsequent sales volumes. Furthermore, since a major determinant of success for people-based training lies in the ability and personality characteristics of the trainees, productivity functions that include these determinants may be more useful predictors.

Productivity analysis is also useful as a companion to life cycle analysis where a number of multiphase or multimedia training programs are involved. As the example in Chapter Six showed, productivity analysis can be used to determine how much of a particular media or approach to use.

While these remarks have suggested certain areas where the different models are likely to be most useful, it really is not possible to provide any types of formulas for their use. As the examples earlier in this chapter illustrated, more than one model is likely to be applied to any particular situation in order to answer different questions. In fact, this leads to one of the firm rules about applying cost/benefits models: You should try to conceptualize your problem in terms of as many different models as possible and then discard those that do not fit or make sense. Following this rule, you are likely to define your problem in the best possible fashion. Remember—there are always many ways of looking at a problem.

The Limits of Cost/Benefits Analysis

This brings us to a consideration of the limitations of cost/benefits analysis. Anyone who engages in planning activity should be well aware of the limitations on their efforts, and this is especially true for cost/benefits analysis. There are three major factors that affect the usefulness of a cost/benefits analysis:

1. The formulation of the problem/model

2. The quantity and quality of the data

3. The inferences and conclusions drawn.

We have already mentioned one of the problems associated with the formulation of the problem—different people may see the problem differently. The conceptualization of the problem determines what variables or parameters will be analyzed. (If an important dimension is left out, then the rest of the modeling activity is of limited value.) When you draw a conclusion that one training approach is more efficient or effective than another, the conclusion is based upon a particular set of variables measured (e.g., resources, training system attributes, skill proficiencies). However, another set of variables might lead you to reach the opposite conclusion. You must always keep in mind the fact that your conclusions are based on what you decided to measure and include in your model.

The second factor is our old friend, Garbage In, Garbage Out. Your conclusions are as good as the data they are based upon. Too little data and data of a dubious accuracy or validity can lead to incorrect results. Unless you take steps to verify and validate the data, you will be at a loss as to its quality. Even knowing that the data are unreliable helps warn you about the limitations of your results.

The third factor has to do with your grasp of what cost/benefits analysis is and how to use it. You should view cost/benefits models as inferential tools, similar to statistics. It is intended to help you understand "what affects what" in a training system, and to aid your judgment in making decisions. Hopefully, you will appreciate that you cannot use the results of cost/benefits models to prove anything. Thus, if a resource requirements model indicates that approach A will save X dollars over approach B, or a benefits analysis suggests that approach A will result in a 10-percent improvement in a specific operational outcome over approach B, you have not proved that approach A is better than approach B! Rather, for the particular way you formulated the model and the data used, approach A will likely save money or improve a certain outcome. If this result seems plausible on the basis of your understanding of the training situation and system, you may make a decision that favors approach A. There is no substitute for expert judgment—cost/benefits models help you sharpen and improve your judgment. They also help make judgments more systematic and objective, and less capricious and subjective. This makes training analysis more of a science and less hocus-pocus.

You should realize that the three factors just discussed are relatively independent. Thus, you can formulate your problem well but collect lousy data or make incorrect inferences. Similarly, you could have good data but use the wrong model. Finally, you could have the right model and good data but simply draw inappropriate conclusions. It follows that to maximize your chances of doing cost/benefits analysis correctly, you should formulate your problem in as many different ways as possible, you should religiously follow the data collection steps outlined in the preceding chapter (particularly the verification and validation step), and you should be circumspect in the inferences you draw as a result of your study. In addition, it is of considerable value (but hard on your ego) to submit each stage of the process to the scrutiny and criticism of colleagues, your spouse, or your worst enemy.

The simple way to assess the utility of your cost/benefits analysis is to ask yourself how well you understand the training situation or system you have been studying. Provided that you answer honestly, you will have a measure of your success. If all you have at the end of a cost/benefits analysis is a bunch of numbers generated by a computer, but no real understanding of the problem or system you are studying, then you should try again or throw in the towel.

Chapter Nine
A Case Study

This chapter presents a case study that illustrates the use of the four major types of models in the same situation. The case study deals with a parts supply company that is about to implement a computer-based ordering system at all of its stores and offices. The training program involves teaching various levels of employees to use the system. This particular training problem is becoming a rather general one in the business and industrial training domain as more and more organizations come to rely on computer systems to conduct their operations. Thus, instead of parts ordering, the system could just as well as have been for customer billing, online banking, retail sales, procurement monitoring, word processing, electronic mail, or many other functions.

The Problem

Acme Parts Supply Company[1] is a medium-sized retail, distributing, and manufacturing organization with about 2,000 employees and 250 stores/offices nation-wide. APS sells directly to the public through its re-

---

[1]All names and events in this case study are quite fictitious (as is true for the entire book.)

tail stores, and sells wholesale to other manufacturers or retailers from its branch offices. The company makes about half of the products it sells at a central plant/warehouse located in Missouri, and ships to all of its stores and customers from this location.

During the past year, APS has been trying out a computer-based ordering system called OATS (Order Administration and Tracking System) at four stores in Missouri, connected to the plant. OATS allows store employees to place, cancel, or check the status of an order immediately. OATS also allows store and company managers to check inventory and sales volumes, and to make thirty-, sixty-, or ninety-day cash flow projections based on the available data. In addition, OATS is used by the plant production supervisors and managers to plan and schedule their manufacturing runs. OATS has dramatically improved the overall efficiency of the four stores in the tryout such that they are filling more orders faster and with greater customer satisfaction than ever before. Thus, the company has decided to go ahead with a full-scale implementation of OATS at all 250 stores and offices.

User training for OATS was handled in small groups (four to five people) and done by the developers of the system (who were outside contractors). It consisted of four morning or afternoon sessions for a total of about twelve hours per person. The training was customized to the needs of the particular group being trained (i.e., store clerks, managers, production supervisors) and consisted mostly of "hands on" practice at the terminals. While lesson plans and job aids were used, no formal training materials or program were developed.

You are hired as a training manager by APS with the development of a company-wide training program for OATS as your major responsibility. APS would like to put all 250 stores and offices online as quickly as possible, although they realize that it may take some time to train everyone how to use the system. You have about three months to formulate the best approach to OATS training, at which time installation of the terminals is scheduled to begin. (Implementation is expected to take about six months to complete.)

Scenario 1: Resource Requirements Model

After preliminary study of the problem, you distinguish between the immediate need (to train approximately 1,000 people in six months) and a long-term need (to train new employees on an ongoing basis). While you must deal with the immediate need first, you also must develop an approach for the long-term need as well. Basically, you have four alternative approaches to consider (see Figure 9–1):

1. You can develop a central training facility (i.e., "school") and conduct the instructions via the traditional classroom approach.

2. You can have individualized instruction (i.e., self-study) at a central learning center.

3. You can conduct the training via small groups in the offices/stores.

4. You can have individualized on-the-job training (OJT).

Because of the large number of people to be trained (about 1,000), the centralized approach (which involves travel costs for each individual) does not appear feasible for the initial training. (Consider that 1,000 trainees with an average travel expense of $500 is $500,000.) Furthermore, no central training facility currently exists at APS, and this would have to be developed at considerable cost. The decentralized group approach would involve sending instructors out to the offices and stores to conduct local training classes. The decentralized individualized approach

TRAINING LOCATION

	Centralized	Decentralized
Group	Classroom	Small Group
Individualized	Learning Center	OJT

TRAINING MODE

Figure 9-1   Alternative Training Approaches

would involve developing a self-study curriculum that could be used for OJT. You reason that this latter approach would probably work well if some people at each location already knew how to use the system (and could therefore provide help), but it is not a good approach for the initial training. Thus, you narrow down your choice to the decentralized group approach for the initial OATS training and the decentralized individualized approach as the likely candidate for long-term OATS training.

Having made this decision, you now have to decide exactly how to implement the decentralized training. APS divides its offices and stores into four major regions: Eastern, Central, Western, and Southern. Each region is scheduled to have approximately ten OATS terminals come on-line per month for each of six months (sixty total). Thus, there is a need to train about forty employees per month in each of the four regions. It appears that two classes per week (one in the morning and one in the afternoon) at a different office or branch location each week (i.e., four different locations per month) would meet the training needs for each region. While this means that some employees will have to travel to other locations for their training, in no case is the distance more than a two-hour drive.

You now have a good idea of your training resource requirements. You will need four instructors (one for each region) who will spend six months "on the road" giving OATS training at a different location each week. They will require some portable terminals (a single branch might only have one—not enough for a class of four or five). Instructor and student guides will need to be developed, which include any necessary overheads, handouts, job aids, etc. In addition, arrangements will need to be made at each office or store location for a room in which the training can be conducted. Of course, the training schedule must be coordinated with the OATS implementation schedule.

Figure 9–2 shows the costs of this training program in the form of a resource requirements matrix. The costs consist of the following:

1. You contract with an instructional development firm ($40,000) to conduct a job/task analysis for OATS training and design/develop an appropriate program and curriculum (including instructor and student guides). This contract also includes the collection of job performance

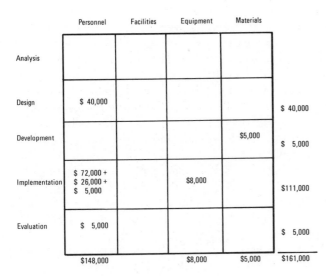

	Personnel	Facilities	Equipment	Materials	
Analysis					
Design	$ 40,000				$ 40,000
Development				$5,000	$ 5,000
Implementation	$ 72,000 + $ 26,000 + $ 5,000		$8,000		$111,000
Evaluation	$ 5,000				$ 5,000
	$148,000		$8,000	$5,000	$161,000

Figure 9-2 OATS Training Costs

data after the system is fully implemented and recommendations for subsequent training (this is an additional $5,000).

2. The printing, packaging, and distribution of the training materials to 250 branches amounts to $5,000.

3. The salaries of the four instructors for seven months (the first month is spent training) is $72,000. Their travel and per diem expense total $26,000.

4. Travel costs of employees totals $5,000.

5. The rental costs of eight portable terminals for six months is $8,000.

There are no special facility costs for training since the classes will use existing office or store meeting rooms. All of the other costs associated with OATS (terminals, telecommunication charges, usage, etc.) are considered as operational rather than training expenses.

Now that you have a plan for the initial training and since you are anxious to get started as soon as possible, you ask for a meeting of the

133

management committee to get approval. While the committee unanimously approves of your approach, they are unwilling to spend more than $100,000 on the initial OATS training. They direct you to cut your costs by $61,000 and then implement your plan.

An obvious cost cutting step would be to eliminate the formal analysis, design, development, and evaluation of the training program and have this done by the instructors. This would save a total of $50,000. However, this would mean that you would have no assurances that what is taught is relevant to the job needs (the role of the job/task analysis), as well as no control over the consistency or quality of the training (the role of the instructor and student guides). Furthermore, without the formal evaluation of job performance, you will have no idea of how well your training worked and how to improve it. So, you conclude that you will not eliminate this aspect of the program.

The only possibility that you see is to double the class size and conduct the training in three months instead of six. This would reduce your instructor salaries and expenses by a total of $45,000. However, it would double employee travel costs from $5,000 to $10,000 since about twice as many employees would have to travel to another office or store for the training. You would now need to lease portable terminals for three months instead of six, but you will need twice as many, so this cost stays the same.

The three-month plan, however, only really makes sense if the installation of the terminals can be speeded up. You call the program manager in charge of the OATS implementation and discuss your problem with her. As it turns out, all of the terminals could be installed in three months, but it was planned for six to allow enough training time! Furthermore, installation of the terminals three months earlier would produce greater cost benefits for OATS since the benefits could be achieved earlier. You make another presentation to the management committee (with the OATS manager present) requesting $121,000 for the three-month training plan. You point out that although you need $21,000 more than the ceiling imposed, the benefits from implementing OATS three months earlier result in substantially greater cost savings (in the order of $50,000). On the basis of the argument that the net savings of an earlier OATS implementation will make up for the extra training costs, your proposal is accepted and you proceed with initial OATS training.

Scenario 2: Life Cycle Costs

Now that you have the immediate training problem under control, you turn your attention to long-term OATS training needs. There are two different needs: new user training and upgrade training (for all systems users). Accounting for turnover and expected growth, you will need to train about 150 new employees each year on OATS. Of the four approaches outlined in Figure 9–1, the centralized group approach seems most appropriate for new user training, since the total number to be trained is relatively small and the training will be distributed over time (i.e., not all employees will leave or join at the same time). The annual costs associated with centralized new user training are:

Student Expenses:	150 × $650 =	$97,500
Instructor Salary:		$30,000
Facilities Operation:		$12,000
Equipment (5 OATS terminals):		$6,000
	Total	$145,500

Upgrade training involves teaching new capabilities or features of the system to all users. While it is possible to simply send out documentation describing such upgrades, data show that few people will take the time needed to study and practice the new features. Thus, potential improvements in system use and operations would not be realized because of lack of explicit and formal training on the upgrades. In the first two years of the system, two major enhancements will be made to OATS. The first is scheduled at the end of six months, while the second is at the end of twelve months. Thus, all users will need upgrade training (lasting about three hours) at six and twelve months after initial implementation. Clearly, any form of centralized training is not feasible, given the number of employees involved. The best approach appears to be the same one used for the initial OATS training, i.e., sending four instructors on the road to give the upgrade training at the offices and stores. This time the instructors will only spend one day at each location and visit more locations. The instructor salary costs for two months (includes their training) will be $20,000. The travel and per diem costs for all four instructors will be $32,000. An instructor's guide will be developed by the regular OATS instructor and documentation on the upgrades will be provided by the

OATS systems group. Thus, the total training cost for each update is $52,000.

You are now able to identify your life cycle costs for the first two years of OATS training (see Figure 9–3). Start-up costs amount to $121,000 for the initial training. The upgrade training costs are actually transition costs (going from one version of the system to another) and amount to $104,000 in total. Steady state costs involve the new user

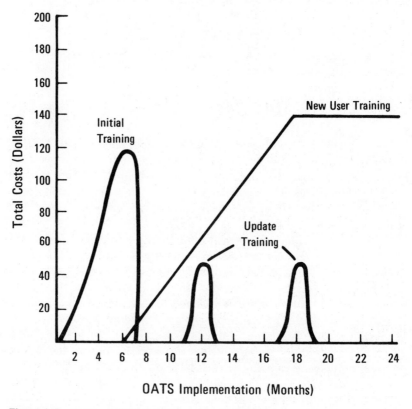

Figure 9-3   Costs of OATS Training

training costs of $145,500 annually. Thus, at the end of a two-year life cycle, the total OATS training costs are:

Total Training = $121,000 + (2 × $52,000) + ($145,500 × 1.5)
Costs (2 years) = $443,250

At the next management committee meeting, you present your plan and figures for long-term OATS training. The committee considers your budget "exorbitant" and insists that you find less expensive approaches to OATS long-term training.

Looking at your proposed costs for both new user and upgrade training, you realize that most of the money is being spent on travel expenses. Clearly, you need to find a training approach that reduces travel costs. Thus, you investigate the possibility of decentralized individualized training. You hire a consultant with experience in the development of multimedia self-study training programs to do a feasibility study and make recommendations. The consultant recommends self-study programs consisting of video, workbook, and online practice exercises be used for new users and upgrade training. The consultant estimates that $150,000 would be needed to design and develop such a program for new used training and $40,000 for each update training program. Another $150,000 would be required to produce and ship the training packages to each location. In addition, you would have to buy a video cassette or videodisc player for each office or store. This would amount to about $125,000 (one-time purchase) plus $10,000 annually for maintenance. The players could be amortized over their five-year expected life span.

The life cycle costs for this approach are:

Total
Training = $121,000 + (2 × $40,000) + ($150,000)
Costs   + 1.5 ($10,000 + $125,000 ÷ 5)
(2 years) = $432,500

While the self-study, multimedia approach only saves $9,750 ($443,250 − $432,500) over the original approach, it involves annual steady state costs of $35,000 ($25,000 + $10,000) for equipment plus the costs of developing and distributing revised versions of the training materials (estimated to be about $30,000 per year) for a total of $65,000, compared to the $145,500 required by the centralized approach. Since the expected lifespan of OATS is at least five years, the total life cycle savings would be:

Total
Life = ($443,250 + 3 × $145,500) − ($433,500 + 3 × $65,000)
Savings = $251,250
(5 years)

In addition, the consultant has presented you with evidence that the self-study multimedia program would require about 25 percent less training time (i.e., three days instead of four) and provide much more effective training because of the individualized instruction.

Armed with this new information, you make a presentation at the next management committee meeting. The committee does not consider the $9,750 reduction in total costs for the first two years to be the kind of substantial cut they were asking for. You insist that if they want APS employees to be well trained to use OATS, it will cost that much money. They say that the company simply cannot afford to spend that much on OATS training. You suggest that the company cannot afford *not* to spend the money on OATS training given its importance. They ask you to support that claim. You take up the challenge.

Scenario 3: Benefits Analysis

To make your case, you initiate three different activities. The first activity is to arrange to have OATS terminals installed in four offices (one in each region) two months ahead of the scheduled training time. You provide them with all of the OATS system documentation as well as the training materials that have now been completed. You want to see how well these branches do with no formal OATS training (but provided with the training materials).

The second activity is to contract with the consultant and the organization that developed the training materials (and is conducting the evaluation) to develop a prototype self-study, multimedia OATS training program and compare it to the instructor approach being used in the initial training. You specifically ask them to investigate the specific contributions made by each of the three major components: the workbook, the video, and the online exercises/testing.

The third activity is to develop a benefits analysis model for OATS training. The model was developed by a task force group consisting of many operational managers, as well as the OATS project manager. A simplified version of the causal model (without weights or coefficients) is shown in Figure 9-4.

The model links up three critical training system attributes (interactive capabilities, presentation capabilities, and data collection capabilities) with one level of training outcomes and four levels of operational outcomes. Interactive capabilities (e.g., feedback) are considered essential for the kind of practice required in OATS training, as well as affecting the type of learning models possible (e.g., realistic simulation of OATS programs). The presentation capabilities (i.e., video, graphics, color, motion, etc.) are also important in terms of the types of learning models possible as well as playing a major role in attitude development/change. The data collection capabilities determine whether the practice and learning models can be adaptive (i.e., instructional strategies based on past performance) and individualized.

The three training outcomes, practice, learning models, and attitudes, affect the first level operational outcomes of proficiency, errors, and usage with OATS. The nature and amount of practice will affect the level of proficiency obtained and the number and type of errors made on the job. The learning models utilized will also affect the proficiency and errors, as well as the way in which OATS is used. The attitudes developed in training will also affect the extent and way in which OATS is used on the job.

All three first-level operational outcomes (proficiency, errors, usage) affect all three second-level operational outcomes (order completion time, order status reporting, and sales/production forecasting). Increased OATS proficiency would reduce the order completion time, improve the order status reporting, and improve sales/production forecasting. Reduced errors while using OATS and increased usage would also have the same effects.

The outcome, order completion time, affects the third-level outcomes, customer satisfaction and total orders processed. Order status reporting affects customer satisfaction (in terms of being able to describe the exact

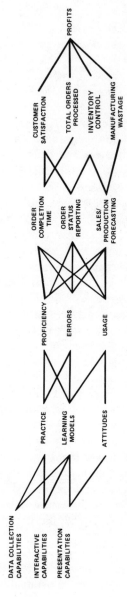

Figure 9-4 Causal Model for OATS Training

status of an order) and inventory control. Sales/production forecasting outcomes also affect inventory control as well as manufacturing wastage. All three of these third-level outcomes affect the fourth-level outcome, profits.

Once this model was developed, the coefficients were assigned by the task force using the delphi method. Next, you and the consultant develop weights for the three major attributes for the instructor-based OATS classes and the self-study, multimedia OATS program being tested. Running the model shows that the self-study program could result in a 1.2-percent increase in profits over the instructor-based approach. (This corresponds to more than 2 million dollars.) With the self-study approach, customer satisfaction is improved, the total orders processed are significantly increased, inventory control is improved, and manufacturing wastage is reduced. You also run the model against a "nontraining" approach that would correspond to simply providing the existing OATS training materials and documentation. This corresponds to a difference of almost 5 percent in reduced profits (about 8 million dollars) over either the instructor-based or self-study, multimedia approaches. A sensitivity analysis shows that the nature and amount of practice is the most important single training outcome influencing operational outcomes.

While you feel that the benefits analysis gives you a fairly strong case for the value of OATS training, as well as the specific benefits of the self-study multimedia approach, you decide to wait for the results of the other two activities prior to going before the committee again.

Scenario 4: Productivity Analysis

By this point, OATS is partially implemented and you have two months of data on the four offices that implemented OATS without training, as well as data on about 150 offices that had training. You randomly select four offices from the 150 and compare the statistics on the average order processing times, usage of the system, number of errors (these are automatically recorded by OATS according to location), and inventory levels. You also call up the managers of the offices to ask about their views of OATS, as well as the regional managers to ask about the performance of the offices. All of the data lead to one clear-cut

141

conclusion. The four offices that lacked training have made little use of OATS and generally have negative attitudes toward the system; the four offices with training have used OATS extensively and their overall productivity has been increased quite significantly. You summarize your data and findings in the form of charts and graphs for presentation.

A few weeks after getting these data, the preliminary results from the self-study prototype study are available. Figure 9–5 displays the data obtained for a comparison of the workbook alone, workbook plus videotape, and workbook, videotape, and online exercises/testing. The data clearly show that each of the three components increases the proficiency obtained. When plotted against development costs for the module developed, Figure 9–6 results, indicating the development cost tradeoffs for different proficiency levels. This figure shows that both video and online exercises and tests produce significant increases in proficiency levels but also increase costs considerably. The benefits analysis can be used to show the detailed effect of this feature in terms of training and operational outcomes.

The study also produces some data bearing on the comparison of the self-study, multimedia approach and the instructor-based approach. As Figure 9–7 shows, training using the prototype self-study module resulted in a skill proficiency level equivalent to that produced after about

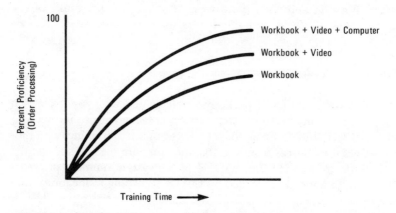

Figure 9-5 Results of OATS Media Comparison Study

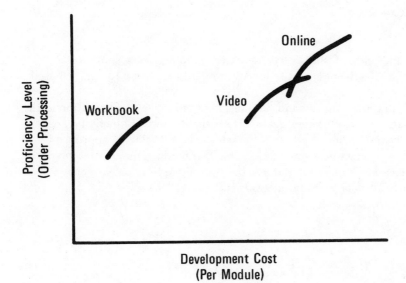

Figure 9-6 Productivity Functions for Different Media

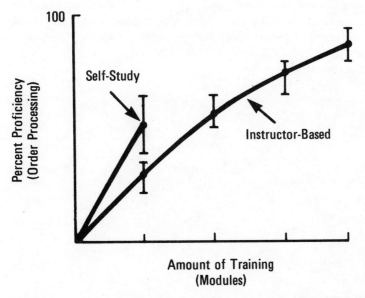

Figure 9-7 Comparison of OATS Self-Study and Instructor-Based Training

143

two modules of the instructor-based training. This supports the improved effectiveness and reduced training time claims for the self-study program.

With these data in hand, you feel ready to make a presentation to the management committee again. The benefits and productivity analysis data have convinced you that the self-study, multimedia approach is the most cost-effective approach for OATS training. You are now prepared to defend this position and ask the committee to approve your plan to implement new user and upgrade training via the self-study multimedia approach.

You Try It

The day of the meeting comes. You present all of your data and make a very convincing case for the importance of OATS training and the effectiveness of the self-study multimedia approach. The project manager for OATS, as well as a number of key operational managers (all of whom served on the benefits analysis task force), unanimously support your plans.

Finish the case study.

Chapter Ten

Ad Hoc Models and Other Approaches

In the preceding chapter, we considered a case study that illustrated the use of the four basic models described in this book. In some situations, an *ad hoc* model made up specifically to deal with the circumstances of a problem will be more useful than these models. Furthermore, some instructional domains (such as public education or equipment simulations) involve special cost/benefit approaches. This chapter discusses such *ad hoc* models and other approaches in the context of examples that illustrate their use.

Improved Productivity: Speed Reading[1]

You are the training director of a large corporation. While reading an article on what managers do with their time, you note that most managers spend about half their time in some kind of reading activity. The

---

[1]This example was inspired by F. Fauley, "Cost Models: A Study in Persuasion," *Training and Development Journal* (June 1975):3–8.

lightbulb goes on—if you can improve the reading speed of your managers, you can probably increase their productivity.

You investigate a number of speed-reading courses. From the available data, it appears that after successful completion of one of these courses, participants are always able to at least double their reading speed for all types of reading materials. You decide to develop a cost/benefits model to determine what kind of ROI speed-reading training would result in. To begin with, you identify your assumptions:

1. Each manager spends approximately four hours per day reading, every work day.

2. As a result of the course, every manager will at least double his or her reading speed.

Next, you define the data needed:

1. How many managers will participate?

2. Where will the course be given?

3. How long will the course be?

4. How much will the course cost?

After evaluation of several available courses and discussions with the companies who give them, you decide upon the following approach. The same one-day course will be given to ten top managers in each of 270 branch offices. The costs will be $75 per manager, as well as average travel expense for the instructor of $500 per branch. In addition to these direct costs, you will have to foot the bill for one day of each manager's salary while taking the course charged to your training budget. The value of one day averages $100. Thus, the costs of the speed reading training are:

Direct:	270 managers × $75/day	= $20,250
	27 trips × $500/trip	= 13,500
Indirect:	270 managers × $100/day	= 27,000
		Total $60,750

As a consequence of this training, you expect to reduce their daily reading time (four hours per day) in half. The annual value of this time savings is:

270 managers × 2 hours × $12.50/hour	= $ 6,750/day
240 days/year × $6,750/day	= $1,620,000/year

For all 270 managers, you expect to realize a savings equal to $1,620,000 per year as a result of this training. This corresponds to an ROI of $1,620,000 ÷ $60,750 = 26.6. Not bad!

In fact, you are so impressed with the whole idea that you present it to your boss (VP of Operations) the next morning. While he is receptive to the idea, he points out a major flaw in your assumption—that all managers who take the course will not continue to speed read regularly (even though they successfully complete the course). He also suggests that it might be a better idea to have the expertise to give the course in-house rather than have to always rely on outside instructors. You promise to examine his objections and report back to him. Exit stage right (gracefully).

You need to collect more data. By following up on organizations who have taken the courses, you discover that only about 10 percent of those who complete the training will continue to use it on a regular basis. You also obtain cost information on an approach that involves sending training specialists from each branch to the course and then having them return and give it to the managers of their own branch. Training instructors to give the course takes three days, costs $350 per instructor, and involves an average of $500 in travel expenses. In addition, you have as indirect costs, the salaries of the managers and trainers for the day the course is given. Thus, total costs associated with this approach are:

Direct Costs:		
27 trainers × $350	=	$ 9,450
27 trips × $500/trip	=	13,500
Indirect Costs:		
270 managers × $100/day	=	27,000
27 trainers × 4 days × $100/day	=	10,800
	Total	$60,750

Since you now expect only ten percent of the managers to actually use the skill on a regular basis, the annual value of the time savings is $1,620,000 \times .10 = \$162,000$. Thus, the ROI for the speed reading course is $162,000 \div \$60,750 = 2.7$ instead of the 26.6 originally computed—still respectable and worth pursuing.

However, you have a dilemma in terms of the two alternative approaches—they both cost the same. To make a decision, you examine the tradeoffs between the two:

Outside Vendor	*In-House Trainers*
1. Expert	1. Credibility
2. Standardized	2. Can give again
3. Recommendations	3. Job enhancement

In the case of the outside vendor, the advantages are that they are experts in the field and in giving the course, that they would be consistent in their presentations, and that they could provide recommendations for making the course work in the organization or with specific individuals. On the other hand, the in-house trainers have credibility with the managers (the "one of us" syndrome), can give the seminar again, and experience job enhancement as a consequence of the training. Clearly, the choice is a close one. Under the circumstances, you would probably go with the in-house approach since that is what your boss suggested—a perfectly good selection on political grounds.

Cost Avoidance: Reducing Employee Turnover[2]

Once again you are the training director of a large corporation. It has been brought to your attention that the high level of turnover (about 25 percent) in the company's Data Processing (DP) divisions is causing bad morale, not to mention wasting a lot of money in recruitment costs.

---

[2]This example was suggested by J. T. Horrigan, "The Effects of Training on Turnover: A Cost Justification Model," *Training and Development Journal* (July 1979):3–7.

After studying the problem for a few weeks, you uncover the following significant data:

	No. Employees	Annual Turnover
Participation in Training/ Education Activities	300	10% (30)
Don't participate in Training/ Education Activities	300	40% (120)
	600	25% (150)

Thus, there is a whopping 30-percent difference in turnover between those who participate in company training and education activities versus those who do not. You conclude that by increasing the number of DP employees who participate, you could substantially reduce the turnover rate.

You set a target of increasing participation from its current level of 50 percent to 75 percent for next year. Thus, instead of 300 participating in T&E activities, next year there will be 450. Assuming the same kind of turnover statistics, you will lose 10 percent of those who take the training (i.e., $450 \times .10 = 45$) and 40 percent of those who do not ($150 \times .40 = 60$), for a total of 105 DP employees projected to quit next year. This compares to 150 this year, for a reduction of 45 employees.

The costs are as follows. The average duration of T&E is ten days. Since the average salary for a DP employee is $100/day, this amounts to a cost of $10 \times \$100 = \$1,000$ per employee. Since the T&E activities already exist, there are no additional costs due to sending more employees (class sizes are made larger). For the additional 150 employees to be trained, the total value of the time is $\$1,000 \times 150 = \$150,000$ per year.

The personnel department estimates that it costs approximately $5,000 to recruit, relocate, and initiate each new DP employee. Thus, if it is possible to prevent forty-five employees from leaving next year, this amounts to a cost avoidance of $\$5,000 \times 45 = \$225,000$.

Thus, the net effect of increasing participation in T&E activities is to increase the annual training costs by $150,000, but to reduce personnel costs by $225,000, for an annual cost savings of $75,000.

Even though you can show a good justification for increasing participation in T&E activities, there is one problem. At present, participation in T&E programs is entirely voluntary—any DP employee who so desires may take advantage of the programs. Thus, to increase participation, you would need to make it mandatory or find out why half of the employees do not participate. Since the first alternative is too totalitarian for your tastes, you pursue the second option.

Your detective work turns up three principal reasons. The first is that some employees find the available programs irrelevant or not suited to their needs. You identify two new courses needed to address the interests of these employees, as well as modifications to some of the existing programs. The second reason is that many employees (particularly senior ones) simply do not feel they can afford to take the time to attend T&E activities. You identify a new course needed for these employees (i.e., time management), which they agree they would attend. Finally, you discover that some DP employees do not have a high enough level of interest in their jobs or a commitment to the company to care about attending T&E programs. You realize that this group probably represents the highest percentage of employees who quit.

You conclude that to increase the participation rate in T&E programs on a voluntary basis, you will need to develop three new courses and make revisions to existing programs. This will amount to about $60,000 in additional costs for next year. Thus, the total cost of reducing turnover is $150,000 + $60,000 = $210,000 for a cost avoidance of $225,000. This is still a savings of $15,000, but not as impressive as before. However, when the various value-added benefits are taken into account, such as reducing work frustration through training, improved feelings of self-worth and personal achievement due to the training, or having more qualified DP professionals, the savings seem quite worthwhile.

The Costs of Alcoholism

In your role as training director of a large corporation, the following information is brought to your attention about alcohol-prone employees in the manufacturing division of the company:

1. They are absent an average of ten days more per year than other employees (necessitating temporary replacements).

2. They account for an additional $960 per employee in medical claims.

3. They produce an average of 500 less units per year than other employees.

This amounts to additional costs of:

Replacements due to absenteeism = 10 days × $90/day	= $	900
Additional medical claims	=	960
Reduced production = 500 × $5/unit	=	2,500
	Total	$4,360

per alcoholic employee per year. You decide to examine the cost/benefits of a rehabilitation program.

After studying other programs, you conclude that a five-day course would be needed. You propose to try it out with twenty-five voluntary employees. Since your training costs average $13.88 per hour,[3] the five-day course (forty hours) for twenty-five employees would cost 40 × 25 × $13.88 = $13,880 to develop and deliver. In addition, the employees' time would be charged to training, i.e., 5 days × 25 employees × $90/day = $11,250. Thus the total cost of the training would be $13,880 + $11,250 = $25,130.

The cost savings to be realized from the rehabilitation program would be 25 × $4,360 = $109,000 − $25,130 = $83,870. The ROI would be $109,000 ÷ $25,130 = 4.3.

However, not all of the employees who take the program will be successful in getting rid of their alcohol problem on a permanent basis. Data suggest that only 20 percent of the employees will be successful, in this case only five of the twenty-five employees who take the program. This means that the cost savings to be expected are 5 × $4,360 = $21,800. Since the course will cost $25,130, this amounts to a loss of $3,330 *for the first year*. The five employees will result in the same savings the year after, i.e., $21,800. This means that by the end of the second year, the program will have resulted in a savings of $21,800 − $3,330 (first year loss) = $17,470. In fact, even if just one employee is "cured" on a per-

---

[3] Total training department budget is $800,000 and 57,760 hours of training are provided for an average cost of $800,000 ÷ 57,760 = $13.88/employee hour.

manent basis, a cost savings will result in the second year ($4,360 − $4,440 = $1,030).

It is instructive to note the cost savings that comprise the $4,360 consist of a cost displacement (the replacement salaries), a cost avoidance (the extra medical claims), and a value-added benefit (the regained productivity).

Costing Higher Education: Chinese Calligraphy

This example illustrates cost analysis measures that are commonly used in the educational realm: costs-per-student and Full Time Equivalents (FTEs). Cost-per-student is computed by dividing the total dollar amount of an instructional program divided by the total number of students per year, per semester, etc. FTE refers to the total number of credit hours associated with a particular course or curriculum. Costs can be expressed in FTEs by dividing the total dollar amounts by the number of hours that define a course or school term for a student.

Our example deals with a Professor I. Ching who teaches a course in Chinese calligraphy at Preppie Arms College.[4] The course is very popular but enrollment must be limited to ten students per semester due to the nature of the instruction. The college has threatened to cut the course because of its high cost-per-student, saying that it is "unprofitable."

Professor Ching decides to investigate the use of video cassettes to increase the class size to forty but still provide the kind of instruction and practice needed for calligraphy. He concludes that the video cassette approach would work fine if the costs are favorable.

The current course is ten contact hours and represents a cost of $30,000 (Ching's annual salary) ÷ 10 = $3,000 per contact hour. Since the course represents three credit hours, the total course cost is $3,000 × 3 = $9,000. The course represents 3 credit hours × 10 students = 30 student contact hours. The cost/student credit hour is $9,000 ÷ 30 = $300.

---

[4]This example is based loosely on J. P. Kielt and D. R. Spitzer, "Costing Educational Technology: Some Promising Approaches," *Educational Technology* (March 1975):42–45.

The video cassette version of the course involves the development of ten cassettes and the acquisition of forty video cassette players. In addition, the equipment involves maintenance costs. The costs amortized over two years are as follows:

Video cassette development (10 segments)	= $120,000
40 players at $500 each	= 20,000
Maintenance (40 × $100)	= 4,000
Total (2 years)	$144,000

Per semester: $144,000 \div 6 = \$24,000$
(6 semesters = 2 years)

The total cost of the video cassette approach is the cost of the development and equipment ($24,000 per semester) as well as Ching's salary for the course ($9,000), i.e., $24,000 + $9,000 = $33,000. The cost-per-student credit hour for the video cassette approach is $33,000 \div (40 \times 3) = \$275$. Thus, even though the class size increases from ten to forty with this approach, the cost-per-student credit hour drops from $300 to $275.

The cost calculation can also be done in terms of FTEs. A FTE at the college is equivalent to ten credit hours. The original version of the calligraphy course equaled (3 credit hours × 10 students) thirty student credit hours or three FTEs. The video cassette version of the course is equal to (3 × 40) 120 student credit hours or twelve FTEs. Thus, the new version of the course is worth an additional nine FTEs, which is worth .9 × 30,000 = $27,000 in terms of Ching's annual salary. Since the cost of the new course is $24,000 per semester, the total savings is $27,000 − $24,000 = $3,000 per semester.

Simulators and Trainers

A large proportion of military and industrial training deals with teaching people how to operate or maintain expensive and often dangerous equipment. This includes aircraft, submarines, tanks, buses, trains, bulldozers, radar equipment, nuclear plants, oil refineries, and a host of factory machinery and manufacturing equipment. In many cases, it makes sense (as well as cents) to use a specially designed trainer or simulator for this type of training rather than the actual equipment itself. In general, trainers and simulators cost substantially less than the actual equipment, and, given that they result in the same learning outcomes, they can result in training cost savings.

The critical part is to be able to show that the use of a simulator will indeed produce on-the-job performance that is as good as training done with the actual equipment. The traditional approach to this issue is based on the notion of *transfer of training*. The idea is as follows. If one group of students who follow a certain training approach show better performance on a criterion task (i.e., fewer errors, less time to learn, faster performance, more accuracy, etc.) than a group who did not have any training (the control group), then the training approach is said to produce transfer. The amount of transfer is a ratio (i.e., percentage) of how much better the trained group does to the control group on the criterion task, and is given by the following formula:

$$\text{Percentage transfer} = \frac{C - T}{C} \times 100$$

where C is the performance measure of the control group on the criterion task, and T is the performance measure of the group receiving training on the criterion task.

For example, suppose that a group of pilots is able to learn how to perform a certain flying maneuver satisfactorily after four hours in a simulator; however, it takes ten hours to acquire this skill without the benefit of the simulator experience. We can compute the percentage of transfer of the simulator as:

$$\frac{10 - 4}{10} \times 100 = 60 \text{ percent}$$

which can be interpreted to mean that the simulator results in 60 percent greater learning transfer than no simulator. Thus, if the cost of an airplane is $4,000 per hour (e.g., a 747), and the cost of the simulator is $400 per hour, we will be saving:

$$(\$40,000/\text{hour} \times 10 \text{ hours}) - (\$400/\text{hour} \times 4 \text{ hours}) = \$38,400$$

by using the simulator.

154

One problem with this simplistic way of assessing simulator effectiveness is that it does not take into account the "diminishing returns" aspect of using a simulator. Normally, a simulator will have its greatest effect in its initial use and its value will diminish with continual use. To account for this, a Cumulative Transfer Effectiveness Function (CTER) is often calculated according to the following equation:

$$\text{CTER} = \frac{C - T}{X}$$

where C is the performance measure of the control group on the criterion task, T is the performance measure of the group receiving training on the criterion task, and X is the performance score of the group in the training task. The CTER allows us to measure the cumulative value of a simulator in different stages of training.

To use our previous example, suppose that if after four hours of prior simulator training, pilots were able to learn the maneuver in four hours in the airplane relative to ten hours without the use of the trainer. The CTER for four hours of training would be:

$$\text{CTER (4 hours):} \frac{10 - 4}{4} = 1.5 \text{ hour/hour}$$

which means that one hour in the simulator is worth one and one-half hours in the airplane after the first four hours. Suppose that after eight hours of simulator training, pilots only required two hours of airplane time. The CTER is now:

$$\text{CTER (8 hours):} \frac{10 - 2}{8} = 1 \text{ hour/hour}$$

i.e., one hour of simulator is equal to one hour in the airplane. If after twelve hours of simulator training, the pilots require one hour of airplane time, the CTER is:

$$\text{CTER (12 hours):} \frac{10 - 1}{12} = .75 \text{ hour/hour}$$

or one hour in the simulator is equal to three-fourths of an hour in the airplane. If the airplane cost is $4,000/hour and the simulator is $400, we would still be saving money until the CTER equalled .10.

The calculation of simulator cost/effectiveness has become a fairly developed subfield of training cost analyses and the foregoing is meant only to convey the basic idea of this approach. You should consult the literature in this area if you wish to pursue this type of cost/benefits analysis.

Summary

In this chapter, you have been introduced to a number of examples illustrating *ad hoc* models and other approaches to cost/benefits analysis in training systems. Actually all of these examples are really abbreviated or mixed forms of the four basic models you have learned. The speed reading, turnover, alcoholism, and Chinese calligraphy examples are all basically resource requirements models, with only a few components included. The alcoholism and calligraphy examples contain multiple-year justifications and, hence, have elements of a life cycle model. Implicit in all of these examples are connections between training system parameters and training or job benefits—the essence of a benefits analysis. Finally, the transfer functions underlying the calculation of simulator cost effectiveness are a special case of productivity analysis.

After examining a number of training cost/benefits studies, you would probably reach the conclusion that there are as many different cost/benefits models and approaches as there are different studies. While there is really nothing wrong with "reinventing the wheel" each time a cost/benefits analysis is to be conducted, it is not a very efficient use of a training manager's time (plus an occasional square wheel gets invented). The standardization of cost/benefits methodology in the training domain (along the lines outlined in this book) could improve the efficiency, effectiveness, and productivity of training managers who conduct cost/benefits analyses.

Chapter Eleven

Computer-Based Instruction

In the previous two chapters, we have looked at a case study that illustrated the four basic models and a series of examples that showed the use of *ad hoc* models and other approaches to cost/benefits analysis. In this chapter, you will study the cost/benefits associated with a particular instructional delivery system, namely, Computer-Based Instruction (CBI). Since a great deal of cost/benefits analysis is concerned with assessing the value of instructional technology (e.g., CBI, videotape/disc, teleconferencing, videotex, microfiche, slide/tape, etc.), it is important to be familiar with the type of considerations involved.

Assumptions in CBI Cost Analyses

In any cost/benefits analysis, the assumptions underlying the calculations are the critical factors that affect the validity and acceptance of the analysis. In cost/benefits studies of CBI (and instructional technology generally), there are three major categories of assumptions: (1) the components to be included in the analysis, (2) the degree of usage, and (3) the life spans of the CBI components. We will discuss each of these.

Components Included

The costs of a CBI system can be broken down into four major components: hardware, software, courseware, and humanware, each of which has an acquisition and ongoing aspect. *Hardware* consists of the CPU, display terminals, peripherals (such as printers or disk drives), and telecommunications equipment (i.e., modems or network controllers). Hardware acquisition costs are those associated with purchase and installation of the equipment; the ongoing costs involve the power and spare parts required.

Software components involve the programs that are used to develop, run, or maintain the system, i.e., the operating system, utility programs, and the authoring languages in which the instructional programs are written. *Courseware* is the term used to refer to the programs that represent the content and delivery of the instruction. Acquisition costs for software and courseware involve the initial cost of programs. However, most courseware is developed from scratch for a particular training need and, hence, acquisition costs are those associated with the development, programming, and testing ("debugging") of courseware.

Humanware costs represent the salaries of all the people involved in a CBI system. This includes equipment technicians who operate and maintain the hardware; programmers and systems analysts who write, implement, and maintain software/courseware; instructional technologists who design and develop courseware; and proctors or instructors who administer the instruction. Almost all human costs are ongoing costs (i.e., salaries); very little is spent on acquisition (i.e., recruitment).

There is one other cost component that does not fit into any of these categories, and this is the ongoing costs of telecommunications. This usually amounts to telephone charges proportional to the amount of usage involved. In some CBI systems in which long-distance communications is required, telecommunication costs can be substantial.

Although the hardware costs are usually the most visible cost of CBI, it is usually courseware and humanware costs that represent the largest cost component of a CBI system. In particular, the development of courseware is very expensive relative to most other media, requiring in the order of 100–400 hours of development time for every hour of instruction produced. Thus, if a cost analysis is conducted that does not fully include courseware development costs, it is likely that the major cost component has been left out.

It should be noted that the components just discussed are generally in addition to (or instead of) the components we have discussed for resource requirements models. Thus, facilities and materials will be required. Analysis and evaluation activities will still be needed. However, the personnel and equipment resources and the design, development, and implementation stages will be significantly diffferent in their composition as just discussed.

One of the ways in which CBI and technology-based instruction differs from traditional classroom-based instruction is that it involves high capital costs (for hardware and courseware development) but relatively low ongoing or operating costs. For this reason, the extent to which use of the system can be spread out over students and time is a critical aspect of a CBI cost analysis.

Degree of Usage

Let's look at degree of student use first. The number of students who use a CBI system is a function of its availability. Suppose that we have a CBI system that consists of eight terminals and costs $24,000 to operate (i.e., $3,000 per terminal). If we assume that the system will be used six hours a day, five days a week, eight months of the year, the total use is:

6 hours × 20 days × 8 months = 960 hours/year

This means that the cost of CBI is $3,000 ÷ 960 = $3.13/student hour.

However, if we assume that the terminals will be used eight hours per day, six days a week, for ten months, the total use is:

8 hours × 24 days × 10 months = 1920 hours/year

or a cost of $3,000 ÷ 1920 = $1.56/student hour.

Finally, if we assume a usage of twelve hours per day, seven days a week, and twelve months of the year, the total use is:

12 hours $\times$ 28 days $\times$ 12 months = 4032 hours/year

corresponding to a cost of $3,000 ÷ 4032 = $0.74/student hour.

Thus, by making different assumptions regarding system use, the per-student-hour cost can be significantly altered. However, all of these calculations assume that the terminals will be fully utilized all of the time they are available. For a variety of reasons (i.e., poor scheduling, broken hardware, or system downtime), this is an unrealistic assumption. In fact, data show that most CBI systems have utilization rates of about 50 percent, i.e., they are only used about half of the time they are available. Utilization rate is obviously an important factor to be taken into account in computing the degree of usage.

Another important factor to be considered is the number of classes or institutions sharing the same courseware. Clearly, if the same program can be used by many classes at many sites, the student usage is increased and the per-student-costs are lowered. A number of CBI systems have successfully shared courseware on a large scale (e.g., the PLATO system) and, hence, the costs of the system can be "spread out" across many more students.

Lifespans

Another assumption made about CBI systems is their lifespan. Thus, the costs of hardware and courseware amortized over a certain estimated life cycle. The problem is, these life cycles are often not realistic. Because of the rapid pace of computer technology, most hardware (and the associated software) has an effective life of four or five years before it is obsolete. Except in unusual cases, most courseware has even a shorter lifetime—usually two or three years. Even relatively stable curriculum, such as basic sales training, safety training, customer relations training, etc., needs to be changed as different approaches or methods come and go, or to stay in line with organizational policies or procedures. You will often find much longer life cycles being assumed for CBI hardware, software, or courseware. You should examine such assumptions carefully.

Variables Affecting CBI Costs

In addition to the three major categories of assumptions underlying cost analyses of CBI, there are four sets of variables that affect CBI costs: the type of system, the type of CBI, the sophistication of the instruction, and the type of students. Each of these variables can substantially affect the cost of CBI.

Type of System

CBI can be provided via many different types of hardware and software systems. Historically, CBI was delivered by means of a time-sharing network in which many display terminals (CRTs) shared the same central computer. More recently, CBI has been delivered by stand-alone terminals (i.e., microcomputers). These two different approaches have quite different financial implications. In a time-sharing system, the initial cost of the system is high, however, additional terminals can be added for relatively little money. With stand-alone systems, the cost of each machine is relatively small, so a small number of terminals can be bought for far less than a time-sharing system. However, since the cost of each stand-alone terminal added is about the same, buying a lot of terminals gets quite expensive (see Figure 11–1).

For example, suppose a time-shared system costs $40,000 and each display unit is $1,000. The cost of a one-terminal system is $40,000 + $1,000 = $41,000. The cost of a ten-terminal system would be $40,000 + $10,000 = $50,000, and the cost of a twenty-terminal system would be $40,000 + 20,000 = $60,000. Now consider a stand-alone system in which terminals cost $5,000 each. A one-terminal system would be $5,000; a ten-terminal system would cost $50,000; and a twenty-terminal system would be $100,000. Thus, under ten terminals, the stand-alone systems are less expensive; over ten terminals, the time-sharing system has a lower per-unit cost.

Today, a third system alternative is available—distributed network systems. Distributed networks consist of stand-alone (so-called "intelligent") terminals that can share data (i.e., courseware or student records) by means of communications links. Such distributed systems are essentially a hybrid of time-shared and stand-alone systems.

161

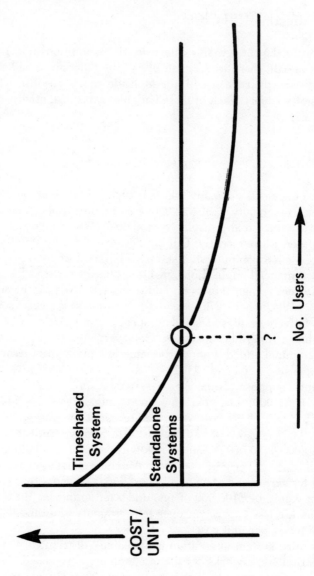

Figure 11-1 Cost Tradeoff for Timeshared versus Standalone Systems

Another cost aspect of the type of system is whether it is dedicated solely to CBI activities or whether CBI is "piggybacked" on a computer system already in use for another purpose (e.g., administrative functions). With piggyback CBI systems, many of the hardware, software, and humanware costs do not need to be attributed to the costs of CBI, since they would exist anyway. The only true costs associated with CBI in a piggyback system are the costs of developing courseware and software.

Type of CBI

There are many ways to use computers in instruction, each of which has different costs factors associated with it. Computer-Assisted Testing (CAT) involves the use of computers to deliver and score tests. This could involve relatively inexpensive fixed item tests in which test items are the same for all students (although they can be presented in random orders), or relatively expensive adaptive tests in which individualized tests are generated for each student.

Computer-Managed Instruction (CMI) involves the use of the computer to track and monitor student progress and includes CAT as one aspect. The cost of CMI depends on whether online or offline tests are involved and the extent of the student management, resource scheduling, and report generation capabilities.

Computer-Assisted Instruction (CAI) refers to the use of the computer to actually deliver instruction. This could be relatively simple drills, lengthy tutorials, or socratic dialogs. Generally, drills take much less time (hence, cost less) to develop than tutorial CAI which, in turn, costs less than dialog CAI.

Computer-Assisted Learning (CAL) involves the use of computers as student tools. This can be in the form of simulations or database inquiry systems. Learning to program a computer in order to solve problems is another form of CAL.

In general, the costs of CBI are lowest for CAT and highest for CAL, primarily due to the differences in development costs associated with the different applications. However, there is considerable overlap in costs. As Figure 11–2 shows, the least expensive type of CAL might be cheaper

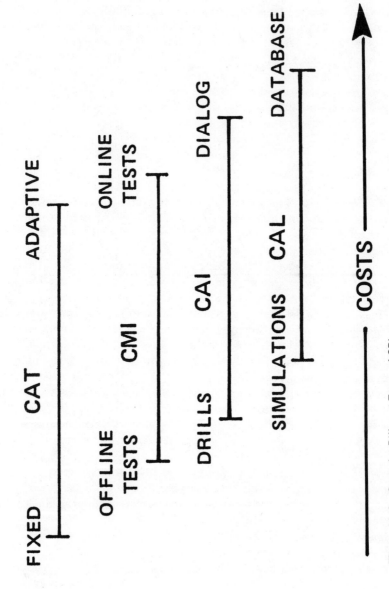

Figure 11-2 Costs for Different Types of CBI

to develop than more expensive types of CAT. This is due to differences in the hardware requirements and courseware development costs associated with the degree of sophistication of the instruction.

Instructional Sophistication

Instructional sophistication refers to the complexity of the programming strategies and interaction capabilities associated with CBI. For example, CAI drills can be based on very simple programming logic in which items are randomly generated and a fixed number of tries is given, or based upon more complex logic in which mistakes lead to specific types of remedial items. Similarly CAT, CMI, and CAL can involve relatively simple or quite complex programming logics, which account for variations in development costs.

Another facet of the degree of instructional sophistication is the nature of the interaction involved. The simplest kind of input consists of single numbers or letters from a keyboard or keypad, and the simplest kind of output is text on a monochrome display. The use of other means of input, such as lightpens, touch panels, or joysticks/mouses, typically requires more costly hardware and greater software/courseware development costs. The use of graphics or color in displays or multimedia (such as videodisc) also increases the hardware, software, and development costs. Speech input or output adds further costs. Thus, as additional input/output features are added to the instruction, the costs tend to increase (see Figure 11–3).

It should be noted that instructional sophistication should not be automatically equated with instructional effectiveness. Many CAT and CMI systems using the simplest of keyboard input and uppercase output have been shown to be quite effective in terms of improving student throughput or in reducing the amounts of instructor time required. Similarly, relatively simple CAI drill-and-practice programs in basic skill areas have been shown to improve skill proficiency. On the other hand, the degree of instructional sophistication possible on a CBI system often limits it to a certain level of usefulness—in general, the more capabilities, the greater the instructional potential of a CBI system.

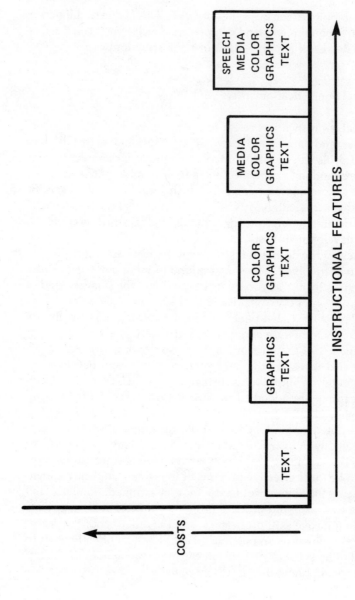

Figure 11-3 Costs and Level of Instructional Sophistication

Type of Students

The type of students involved in the instruction will have a significant impact on the hardware required, the level of instructional sophistication needed, and the cost/benefits case. When developing CBI for young children or the handicapped, capabilities such as color, graphics, touch input, and sound effects are generally desirable. On the other hand, to teach clerks how to use an online ordering system, a simple alphanumeric terminal may be fine. In developing CBI for medical diagnosis or electronics troubleshooting, the instructional presentation logic and answer analysis may be very complex; a tutorial on safety procedures or a drill on basic terminology might be relatively simple.

Different types of students usually cost different average amounts to educate or train. Thus, the cost per student hour for elementary school pupils is typically less than $1, and in the $2–5 range for college undergraduates. However, professional education (e.g., medicine, law, engineering), as well as industrial or military training, is often in excess of $10 per student hour. Similarly, special education for the handicapped or disadvantaged can exceed $10 per student hour. When it comes to making cost justifications for CBI, you can see that it will be much easier to do for military trainees than high school students or handicapped students over college students.

When costing CBI within an organization or institution, you should be sensitive to the fact that different types of students will likely result in different CBI costs. Therefore, if you have the option, you should pursue CBI for the student group that will result in the lowest system costs (hardware, software, courseware), or that will represent the highest per student hour costs in order to produce the most favorable cost justification for CBI.

Illustrative Scenarios

To put the foregoing discussion on assumptions and variables that affect the costs of CBI into perspective, this section discusses four CBI scenarios, each of which represents a different set of considerations. The four scenarios are based on fairly different situations: basic skills education in an elementary school, medical education at a university, maintenance training in the military, and administrative training for a government agency.

Basic Skills/Elementary Education

Consider first a basic skills, elementary education scenario. This involves drill-and-practice programs to teach children arithmetic, spelling, and reading skills. The hardware consists of eight terminals that run off a time-shared system, which the school bought originally for administrative computing. Thus, the CBI is piggybacked on a system whose main purpose is administration rather than instruction. Furthermore, the basic skills courseware was bought from an educational computer consortium at a relatively modest fee. In addition to the CAI programs, there is also a CMI program that allows teachers to automatically generate detailed reports on student progress. The terminals are capable of color and graphics, and these capabilities are fully utilized in the drill-and-practice programs to maintain the interest and attention of the children. The CAI programs are used as adjunctive instruction, i.e., they are used in addition to regular classroom instruction. Each of one hundred students receives an average of about thirty minutes of terminal time per day. In addition to the basic skills drills, there are some games available on the system, and these are used (liberally) as rewards by the teachers. The costs associated with this scenario are:

One-time charge for software/courseware:	$2400
Monthly rental of terminals ($120 × 8):	$960
(includes maintenance)	

Since the system is already funded for administrative functions, the terminal cost represents the only hardware costs.

The total number of student hours per day is 100 × .5 = 50 hours. This amounts to a total of 1,000 student hours/month. If we assume that the software/courseware costs are amortized over two years, the cost is $100/month. Thus, the total monthly cost is $960 + $100 = $1,060. This means that the cost per student hour is $1,060 ÷ 1,000 = $1.06. (This is the approximate cost of instruction at the elementary level.)

Note some of the costs that have been omitted from this calculation. There are facility costs (the room the terminals are located in) and materials costs (e.g., paper for the reports printed). There was also programmer time required to install the programs and make occasional changes requested by teachers. There is also time required to schedule the use of the terminals. On the other hand, students often use the terminals after classes and on Saturdays, increasing the number of hours. In addition, some of the teachers and students have learned to program and write their own programs—an important skill. (See the last section in this chapter.)

Medical Education at a University

In the second scenario, we look at the costs of medical education provided via CBI. This involves many different courses consisting of drills, tutorials, and simulations. The CBI system involves a large time-shared computer used exclusively for CBI at the university. The terminals are high-resolution graphic displays that accept touch input. Twenty terminals are located in a CBI learning center; an additional four terminals are available elsewhere for instructors to author courses or examine student records. In most cases, the courseware represents the major form of instruction (along with labs). Instructors are available in the center during the times scheduled for their courses.

Almost all of the courses were developed at the university (although some were based heavily on successful CBI courses at other universities). Instructors can either learn the authoring language and write the courseware themselves (via online or offline courses), or work with one of the two instructional programmers on the staff of the computer center. The medical facility provides one semester (three months) of time to three instructors per year for the specific purpose of creating/revising CBI courseware. (This can be valued at $8,000—the worth of one semester's salary.) In addition, many instructors work on their courseware during the day, evenings, and weekends.

The use of the computer, running of reports, and all CBI programming or support services all come out of a general computing budget for the medical faculty. This amounts to about $200,000 annually, of which half could be attributed to CBI.

169

To take advantage of the CBI system, the medical faculty had to acquire its own terminals and communication controllers. The total cost of the twenty-four terminals and controllers was $168,000 or $7,000/terminal. This one-time purchase cost is being amortized over four years. In addition, operating and maintenance costs on the equipment amount to $12,000 per year. The computer center is unsupervised, except for the instructors who are present during their classes. (The rule for terminal use is first priority for students of the scheduled class, followed by students of any class, followed by instructors and, finally, students not enrolled in classes.) The annual costs associated with this application are as follows:

Annual terminal cost: $168,000 ÷ 4   = $ 42,000
Annual operating/maintenance cost: 12,000
Annual CBI budget component: 100,000
Annual courseware development: $8000 × 3   =   24,000

Annual total cost $178,000

The CBI center is open seventy-six hours a week. For the twenty terminals, this results in a potential of 1,520 student hours per week. However, the average utilization rate is about 50 percent, for a total of 760 actual student hours per week. For the forty weeks that the center is open in a year, this results in a total of 30,400 student hours annually.

The cost-per-student hour is thus $178,000 ÷ 30,400 = $5.86. For medical education at the university level, this is a very attractive per-student-hour cost. Note that unlike the first example where the CBI was adjunctive (and, hence, an add-on cost to existing costs), in this scenario the CBI provides mainline instruction, i.e., replaces the previous classroom approach.

Maintenance Training in the Military

The third scenario involves maintenance training in the military —specifically learning how to troubleshoot and repair the electronic components of a large variety of satellite communications equipment. This equipment is very expensive and not readily available for training purposes. For this reason, computer simulation of the equipment operation and malfunctions is used for maintenance training. About 50 percent of the entire maintenance training program involves the use of the simulators. This includes almost all of the "hands on" practice and most of the basic principles of training.

The CBI system is a specially engineered, microcomputer-controlled videodisc terminal consisting of two monitors (one for computer-generated instructions and the other for videodisc images). Input devices consist of a keypad and a control knob, which controls cursor position on the display screens. Each terminal also includes a printer and disk drives. There are twelve of these special terminals, each of which cost a total of $240,000 to procure. All of the terminals are located in a training lab along with actual equipment, which is also used in the training program.

An instructor is always present in the lab, which is used eight hours a day, five days a week. The instructor's annual salary is $28,000. The maintenance course is six weeks long, and the trainees spend a total of one hundred hours in the simulation lab.

The courseware for the system consists of a set of three videodiscs, along with the programs that control them (on diskettes). In addition, there is instructional management software that is used to process the student performance data and generate reports. All of this courseware and software (including videodiscs) was developed by a contractor for a total of $450,000.

The lifetime of this CBI system (i.e., hardware/software/courseware) has been established as five years. An annual hardware upgrade and courseware revision allowance of $50,000 has been budgeted. In addition, a technician has been assigned to the maintenance of the system on a half-time basis (annual salary: $18,000). The costs of this system are as follows:

Annual terminal purchase cost: $240,000 ÷ 5	= $ 48,000
Annual courseware development cost: $450,000 ÷ 5	= $ 90,000
Annual upgrade/revision costs:	$ 50,000
Instructor (full time):	$ 28,000
Repair technician (half-time):	$ 9,000
Total annual cost	$225,000

Each class consists of twelve students for six weeks (total of one-hundred terminal hours per student), and there are eight classes per year. Thus, a total of 12 × 100 × 8 = 9,600 student hours are logged annual-

171

ly. This corresponds to a cost per student hour of $225,000 ÷ 9,600 = $23.44. For this kind of highly specialized technical training, this kind of per-student-hour cost is typical.

Administrative Training in a Government Agency

This fourth and last scenario focuses on a CBI used in a government agency to provide administrative training. The terminals and system used for CBI are the same terminals actually used in the administrative activities being taught (records processing and inquiry). Each of the agency's 420 offices across the United States contains from two to six of these terminals, any of which can be used for training purposes if not required for the actual job.

As far as the agency is concerned, the use of terminals and system for training purposes is strictly a "value added" situation, since the equipment would be there anyway. Prior to the use of the system itself for training, it was accomplished via self-study workbooks and a lot of on-the-job training by someone who already understood how to use the system (usually a supervisor). The CBI approach is a lot more effective and requires relatively little on-the-job assistance.

The only real costs associated with the CBI system were the development of the courseware. It was developed by a training analyst and a programmer who worked together for approximately six months to design and implement the five-hour course (a total of 240 person days). It has been estimated that an additional eighty days per year each will be required for courseware revision and update.

An off-the-shelf CBI software system was used, which was leased for $2,400 per year from the computer vendor. In addition, the programmer attended a two-week authoring course, which cost $950 plus expenses of $1,200 (total of $2,150).

The start-up costs of the system are 240 days × $100/day = $24,000 + $2,150 = $26,150. The ongoing operating costs are 80 days × $100/day = $8,000 + $2,400 = $10,400. If the start-up costs are amortized over a five-year period, the annual cost would be $5,230, for a total CBI cost of $10,400 + $5,230 = $15,630. About 800 people are trained to use the system each year, for a cost of $15,630 ÷ 800 = $19.54 each, or $3.91 per student/hour.

The use of CBI has provided many benefits that make it highly valued. The training course is always up to date, since the instruction is changed whenever system changes are made. Previously, the workbooks had been updated only semi-annually. It is now possible for the training department to monitor the progress of individual students and the effectiveness of the trainng via automatically generated reports. With the workbooks, data were hard to obtain and always incomplete. Finally, the employees often use the CBI system as a job aid to refresh themselves on how to do something they have forgotten. Before, they would have had to get help from their supervisor or make (often incorrect) guesses.

Effectiveness and Other Considerations

The discussion in the earlier part of this chapter and the preceding examples have basically been focused on the factors that affect the cost of CBI. This is the kind of information that would be critical to resource requirement and life cycle cost models where the focus is on efficiency and an equal instructional effectiveness assumption is made. CBI systems have commonly been shown to increase efficiency in terms of shorter training durations, greater student throughput with the same level of resources, or reduced resource requirements.

For benefits and productivity models, it is necessary to show increased instructional effectiveness. In many cases, this has been demonstrated. Thus, students have been shown to achieve greater increases in grade point averages or pre-/post-tests, and employees have been shown to produce better on-the-job performance as a result of CBI in comparison with conventional classroom approaches.[1] Not always, mind you. As with any instructional approach, there are good (effective) and bad (inef-

---

[1] Discussions of these studies can be found in the readings listed under "Technology" in the next chapter.

fective) attempts. Putting poor instruction on a computer does not magically make it good instruction!

Despite demonstrations of the cost efficiency and effectiveness of CBI, it has typically received great resistance from the education and training community (not from students, interestingly enough). One problem has been that while CBI may be shown to be much more effective than an existing approach, it also costs more. Educators and trainers have been hard pressed to decide how much it is worth to double or triple instructional effectiveness. Thus, if a CBI system can double initial on-the-job performance (in terms of accuracy or speed), is it worth twice the cost? No one has really been able to answer this question.

A second problem has been that education and training systems are often unable to change in order to maximize or even take advantage of increased efficiency or effectiveness of CBI. For example, CBI normally results in individualized instruction that allows students to progress at their own rate. In most educational systems that are locked into fixed length school terms or semesters, this benefit is of no real value. However, in training systems where the employee can be back on the job performing useful work as soon as the training is completed, reduced training times can pay off. The classic anecdote that comes to mind at this point is the situation that prevailed when a branch of the military initially tried out CBI and individualized instruction. Because the duty assignment system was still geared to fixed duration training courses, trainees who finished early were given guard and KP duty until their duty assignment date. Word soon got around and new trainees made sure that they did not finish early with the CBI system.

A third consideration about the use of CBI is the value of the computer literacy it produces among students or employees. Depending on the type of CBI involved, this literacy ranges from simply becoming comfortable interacting with a computer system to actually understanding how to program a computer or how to use it to access and manipulate information. Given the increasing prevalence of computer systems in modern society and the workplace, being able to comfortably interact with computers is quickly becoming a basic life-coping skill. The contribution of CBI to computer literacy represents a benefit seldom accounted for in CBI cost analyses.

While the issue of efficiency and effectiveness of CBI will probably always be with us, it is likely to significantly diminish in importance as hardware, software, and courseware become cheap enough. Once an instructional technology passes below a certain "tolerable" cost threshold, there is relatively little interest in cost/benefits analysis (except to select the best type of technology). Thus, today one would hardly think of doing a cost/benefits analysis in order to buy a slide/overhead projector or video cassette player. The costs of these technologies (i.e., the hardware and "software") is sufficiently low to bear without elaborate cost/benefits justification. In the near future, the hardware, software, and courseware needed for most CBI applications will be inexpensive enough, and the expectancies regarding interactive, individualized instruction will be such that CBI costs will be accepted in the same fashion.[2]

This does not mean that the need for cost/benefits studies in CBI will totally evaporate. Rather, studies will be needed to compare alternative system configurations and capabilities. The discussion earlier in this chapter outlined some of the variables that would be involved.

Because of the number of assumptions and variables affecting CBI costs, it probably represents one of the most difficult instructional technologies to properly analyze. However, technologies such as video and teleconferencing are equally complex. Yet all of the evidence suggests that education and training activities will become increasingly technology-based. For this reason, it is imperative that we improve the sophistication of our cost/benefit tools in the instructional domain.

---

[2]For further discussion of the concept of tolerable costs, see R. J. Seidel, "It's 1980: Do You Know Where Your Computer Is?" *Phi Delta Kappan* (March 1980): 481–485.

Chapter Twelve

Summing Up

In Chapter Seven, the ten steps in conducting a cost/benefits analysis shown in Figure 12–1 were described. Chapters Two through Six basically dealt with steps 1 and 2. Actually, steps 1 and 2 are very closely intertwined since choosing the model essentially amounts to the definition of the problem. The selection of a particular model defines what view of the problem you take. Steps 3 through 8 were dealt with in Chapter Seven, and steps 9 and 10 were addressed in Chapter Eight. This last chapter summarizes the key concepts of these chapters and discusses assorted problems you will likely encounter in conducting cost/benefits analyses. It also includes a final exercise and suggestions for further reading.

Recapitulation

Chapter One introduced the basic concepts of cost/benefits analysis. This included the distinction between *efficiency, effectiveness,* and *productivity,* and between *cost reduction, cost avoidance,* and *value-added benefit.* The five major steps were outlined: formulating the question or problem, developing a model and assumptions, collecting data, computing the costs and benefits, and using the results.

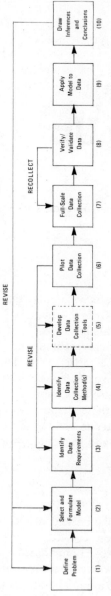

Figure 12-1 Steps in Conducting Cost/Benefits Analysis

In Chapter Two, the four basic models were introduced. Resource requirement models allow the identification of costs associated with each stage of the training cycle according to four major categories of resources: personnel, equipment, facilities, and materials. Life cycle models account for costs in four major phases in the life span of a training program or approach: R&D, startup, operational period, and transition period. Benefits models are used to identify the relationships between training system attributes and training or operational outcomes. Productivity models are based on a function that associates a specific set of training or learning variables with certain performance variables. Resource requirements and life cycle models are useful for determining cost savings and improving cost efficiency. Benefits and productivity models assess improvements in training effectiveness.

Chapter Three described the resource requirements model. Using the resource requirements model involves completing the applicable cells of a resource requirements matrix. By completing matrices for each training approach to be compared, the relative costs and cost savings can be determined. Different training approaches often result in a different pattern of costs in terms of different types of resources needed.

The use of life cycle models were described in Chapter Four. In a life cycle model, the costs of four major phases are computed: R&D, startup, operational (or steady state), and transition. One of the most important considerations in the calculation of life cycle costs is the duration of the start-up and transition periods. The duration affects the potential amount of the cost savings in the operational phase. In most cases, a shorter duration period will result in the greatest cost savings; however, in some situations, a longer duration produces greater savings.

In Chapter Five, benefits analysis was described. Benefits analysis allows you to determine the value of different training system attributes in terms of training and operational outcomes. The crux of benefits analysis is a causal model that identifies the relationships between training system attributes and training or operational outcomes. The validity of the causal model and, hence, the benefits analysis, depends on the validity of the values attached to these relationships.

Productivity analysis was discussed in Chapter Six. A productivity function relates performance measures (e.g., job proficiency levels, achievement scores, students throughput) to training or learning variables (e.g., instructional procedures, technology, amount of practice), which can be associated with requirements (hence, costs). Since productivity analysis deals with increased training outcomes for fewer resources, the concept of return on investment (ROI) is particularly important in this context.

Chapter Seven discussed data collection. Six data collection steps were outlined: (1) identification of the data requirements, (2) identification of the data collection methods, (3) development of data collection tools, (4) pilot data collection, (5) full-scale data collection, and (6) verification/validation of the data. In the course of collecting data, a number of problems are to be anticipated. To reduce these problems, it is important to provide a rationale to all those who contribute data, and ensure that they will receive feedback on the use of the data they provide.

Planning and forecasting was the subject of Chapter Eight. Three kinds of forecasting areas were discussed: predicting the training resources needed; predicting how many trainees will be needed, where, and when; and predicting what kinds of skills will be needed and what backgrounds would be desirable for certain jobs. Different models are suited to different kinds of forecasting—no single model is likely to be used or all three kinds. In addition, different models are more or less suitable for different types of training needs. Finally, the three major limitations of cost benefits models were discussed in terms of formulation of the problem and model, the quantity and quality of the data, and the inferences and conclusions drawn from the modeling results.

Chapter Nine presented a case study that showed how all four major types of models could be applied in the same training situation to answer different questions. The example illustrated how each model required different data and data collection techniques. It also illustrated the ten steps shown in Figure 12–1 in the context of a real application.

In Chapter Ten, *ad hoc* models and other approaches to cost/benefits analysis in training were discussed. *Ad hoc* models, tailored to the needs of a specific training problem, were illustrated by three examples: speed reading, employee turnover, and an alcoholism program. Two different approaches were discussed and illustrated: costing higher education and cost analyses involving simulators or trainers.

Computer-Based Instruction (CBI) was discussed in Chapter Eleven to illustrate the additional considerations associated with the cost/benefits of instructional technology. The chapter outlined the major assumptions and variables that affect the costs of CBI. This included the components covered, the degree of usage assumed, the projected system lifespan, the type of CBI system, and the degree of instructional sophistication. Four scenarios were presented, which showed how these assumptions and variables interact: basic skills/elementary education, medical education at a university, maintenance training in the military, and administrative training in a government agency. Finally, the dimensions of CBI effectiveness were discussed.

We will now go on to discuss obstacles and roadblocks in conducting cost/benefts analysis.

Obstacles and Roadblocks

There are many obstacles that can be encountered while conducting cost/benefits analysis. Some of the major categories are:

1. Lack of time to plan

2. Objections to analysis or modeling

3. Difficulty conceptualizing problem

4. Difficulty collecting data

5. Problems drawing conclusions

6. Lack of acceptance of results.

Many training managers and administrators find it very difficult to budget time to plan and, hence, conduct a cost/benefits analysis. They are too busy dealing with immediate problems ("putting out fires") to have time to think about the future (even if the future is only six months away). This is basically an attitude problem. One of the most important functions of a manager is to plan —although many managers do not realize this. Also, to the extent that a manager does a good job planning, many potential crises and problems will have been foreseen and, hence, less time will be needed for "fire fighting." (Proverbially, "An ounce of prevention is worth a pound of cure.")

In the context of training, it is necessary to anticipate training needs (i.e., programs, curricula, courses, materials, etc.) far enough in advance to study alternatives, formulate models, and collect data. As simple as this sounds, it represents a major problem for many managers. For

181

example, in the case study in the previous chapter, the manager began planning for new user and upgrade training before the system was even implemented. Had the manager waited until this training was needed, there would have been no time to analyze and explore different training approaches. The failure to think about training needs early enough is probably the biggest single obstacle to the use of cost/benefits analysis.

Objections to any type of analysis or modeling effort represents another major category of obstacles. Some people do not believe in any kind of analytic efforts, as expressed by the classic remark, "I don't want studies, I want action!" To some extent, this attitude may be justified—many studies are conducted simply as "busy work" with no real utility. The trick to overcoming this objection is to assure the person that the results of the study will definitely be used as part of a decision-making process. The modeling and data collection procedures should be explained, as well as how the model will be used to reach conclusions. Once someone is convinced that a cost/benefits analysis will result in some useful outcome, her or she will generally withdraw any objections to the analysis.

Another major obstacle is difficulty conceptualizing the problem (i.e., formulating a suitable model). It is sometimes difficult to see past the unique aspects of each problem and recognize the fact that it fits a general model. The key is to focus on the question to be answered (i.e., how to decrease costs, how to improve effectiveness, etc.), and not on the details of the particular training problem being studied, since the question indicates what type of model is appropriate. In order to formulate a model, you must identify the training variables (what factors can be changed or manipulated) and the training outcomes (what results or effects can be produced). The model specifies relationships between the variables and the outcomes. If you are unable to identify variables and outcomes, then you cannot formulate a model. Thus, if you can identify the things that need to be changed, but not the factors that will affect them, then it will be difficult to construct a model. (Of course, you can always make up something and hope eventually to find out what it really is—physicists do this all the time.)

Difficulties collecting data have been discussed in detail in Chapter Seven. Generally, they arise due to one of four types of concerns:

1. The belief that the data will be used against them

2. The belief that the data will be misunderstood

3. The belief that the data will take too long to collect

4. The belief that the data will not be used for anything worthwhile.

Each of these different concerns must be addressed and overcome.

Drawing conclusions about the results of an analysis is another category of problem that occurs. To the extent that the model was formulated to answer a specific question, reaching conclusions should be straightforward. On the other hand, if the original question was not clearly delineated or the model was not closely tied to a specific question, it may be difficult to draw conclusions. Sometimes there may be insufficient data to reach a conclusion, requiring more data collection. Alternatively, there may be adequate data but insufficient analysis of the data. Running many iterations of a model with slight changes each time or on different data sets is often a very tedious task. This is why it is almost essential that any real modeling effort that involves a considerable amount of data be done via computer. Having the data bases and model online usually means that the analysis process can be speeded up.

The last major category of obstacles is lack of acceptance of results. Next to lack of time to plan (and, hence, not conducting cost/benefits analyses), lack of acceptance of a completed analysis is probably the most common obstacle, due to a number of reasons:

1. Failure to acccept model, assumptions, or data

2. Lack of understanding of model

3. Unwillingness to change status quo

4. Lack of participation in the analysis.

People may not accept your formulation of the problem (i.e., the model), the assumptions of the model, or the data used. Each of these is a legitimate concern. You may have conceptualized the problem incorrectly, you may have based the model on incorrect assumptions, or you may have poor data. The only way to avoid these pitfalls is to ensure that you have everyone who might be involved in the decision-making process examine your formulation of the problem and assumptions at the beginning of your analysis, as well as verifying/validating all of the data collected. If you do this and make sure that any disagreements are resolved early in the analysis, you should avoid encountering this problem after the study is completed.

Lack of understanding of the model (and, hence, belief in the results of the analysis) is a frequent problem. It is often difficult to explain a complex model in the relatively short timeframe of a meeting. Thus, it is a good idea to circulate a detailed description of the model and results prior to the meeting so that you can build on and explain this description. In any case, you should prepare a very clear description of the model and how it was applied to the data to produce your results and conclusions. Under no circumstances should you present your results and conclusions without explaining the model—this is inviting rejection of your efforts by someone who does not understand what you are doing. In the context of presenting the results of a cost/benefits analysis, ignorance is not bliss!

Unwillingness to change the status quo, either due to a general resistance to change, or because the change threatens the power of a particular individual or group, is another common reason underlying lack of acceptance. Since it is likely that the conclusion of your analysis is to introduce a new program, approach, or course (which will replace something already in existence), there are bound to be some individuals who oppose the change. If your conclusions are based on sound data and make a good business case for the proposed change, then you can probably survive one or two dissenters. On the other hand, it is much better practice to go over the results with each decision-maker prior to the meeting and deal with objections beforehand.

This brings us to the most surefire antidote to rejection of your results: participation in the study itself. Many people refuse to believe in anything that they have not personally been involved in. Thus, a golden rule of cost/benefits analysis is to involve, in some way, every decision maker who may be affected by the conclusions of your analysis. Simply having them review the plan for the analysis or the final models may be sufficient. Having them assist in the formulation of the model, the data collection, or reaching conclusions is even better. Not only does their involvement ensure their understanding of the model and acceptance of the results, but it is very likely that they will make contributions which improve the analysis. So, a word to the wise: Get as much participation as you can for your analysis.

You Try It

Here is a final exercise to help you think about the discussion in this chapter. Imagine that you are the director of training for a major metropolitan police department. You determine that there is a strong need for some kind of community relations training for the officers in the department. After studying the community relations training done by other police departments, you develop a proposed program. To examine benefits of this program, you develop a benefits model based on data provided by the other departments you studied, as well as input from members of your own department. It is clear from your model that significant benefits in terms of reduction in violent crimes and apprehension of certain types of offenders will result from the program. You develop a formal proposal and are scheduled to make a presentation at the next departmental meeting to seek approval of your plan. Meanwhile, you brief each major decision maker in the department, including the chief and superintendent, on the results of your analysis and proposed plan.

At the meeting, you make a convincing presentation. All members agree that the proposal is sound and that your study clearly outlines the benefits of the training program. However, there are two other items on the meeting agenda. One is a proposal upgrade to the current fleet of squad cars by replacing cars that are barely operational and increasing the total number to meet the minimum demands of the department. Convincing data are shown on the run-down state of the cars and inability of department to respond to emergency calls satisfactorily. The second proposal concerns salary raises for senior officers in the department. The data show that the current salaries are among the lowest of any police department in the nation. Other data show a steady increase in attrition by senior officers, which is leaving the force short-handed in experience. Salary increases are needed urgently.

The members of the board would like to fund all three proposals. Alas, there is only enough money to fund one of the efforts and absolute-

185

ly no possibility of any additional funds for this year's budget. The superintendent asks for suggestions. What would you suggest?

Further Reading

Since this book is intended as a practical guidebook rather than a scholarly work, it contains no discussion of the relative merits of other approaches to cost/benefits analysis. You should be aware, however, that there is considerable literature on the subject. Should you become truly involved in cost/benefits work, you will quickly outgrow the help provided in this book. This section provides you with some suggestions for further reading.

General

There are quite a number of books that have been written on the topic of cost/benefits analysis from different perspectives. Here is a list:

Barsby, S. L. *Cost Benefits Analysis and Manpower Programs.* Lexington, Mass.: D. C. Heath, 1972.

English, J., ed., *Cost-Effectiveness: The Economic Evaluation of Engineered Systems.* New York: Wiley & Sons, 1968.

Fisher, G. H. *Cost Considerations in Systems Analysis.* New York: American Elsevier, 1977.

Kendall, M. G., ed. *Cost-Benefit Analysis.* New York: American Elsevier, 1971.

Layard, R., ed. *Cost-Benefit Analysis.* London: Penguin, 1972.

Maciariello, J. A. *Dynamic Benefit-Cost Analysis.* Lexington, Mass.: D. C. Heath, 1975.

Mishan, E. J. *Cost-Benefit Analysis.* New York: Praeger, 1976.

Seiler, K. *Introduction to Systems Cost Effectiveness.* New York: Wiley Interscience, 1969.

Sugden, R., and Williams, A. *The Principles of Practical Benefit-Cost Analysis.* London: Oxford University Press, 1978.

Thompson, M. S. *Benefit-Cost Analysis for Program Evaluation.* Beverly Hills, Calif.: Sage, 1980.

Wolfe, J. N., ed. *Cost Benefit and Cost Effectiveness: Studies and Analysis.* London: George Allen & Unwin, 1973.

The references in these books will lead you to hundreds of original studies reported in professional journals and magazines.

Training

The literature on cost/benefits analysis in education and training systems is considerably more sparse than the general subject. Actually, quite a lot has been written about cost/benefits analysis in training, however, it is not easily found. The problem is that most of the studies done by private industry, the government or the Department of Defense, are rarely published in public form. Instead, they are issued in the form of technical reports and not very accessible. Some useful readings are:

Braby, R., et al. "A Technique for Choosing Cost-Effective Instructional Delivery Systems." TAEG Report #6, Orlando, Fla.: Navy Training Analysis and Evaluation Group, April 1975.

Carpenter, M. V., and Haggart, S. A. "Cost Effectiveness Analysis for Educational Planning." Rand Report P-4327, Santa Monica, Calif.: Rand Corporation, 1970.

Doughty, P., et al. "Guidelines for Cost Effectiveness for Navy Training and Education." NPRDC Special Report 76-Q-12, San Diego, Calif.: Navy Personnel Research & Development Center, 1976.

Fauley, F. E. "Cost Models: A Study in Persuasion." *Training and Development Journal,* (June 1975):3–8.

Horrigan, J. T. "The Effects of Training on Turnover: A Cost Justification Model." *Training and Development Journal* (July 1979): 3–7.

Orlansky, J., and String, T. "Cost-Effectiveness of Maintenance Simulators for Military Training." Institute for Defense Analysis P-1568, Arlington, VA., August 1981.

Shipp, T. "To Survive the Budget Inquisition, Prove Your Training Makes Dollars and Sense." *Training/HRD* (November 1980): 23–29.

Wilkinson, G. L. "Cost Evaluation of Instructional Strategies." *AVCR* 21 (1972).

Technology

One of the common reasons for conducting a cost/benefits analysis in the training domain is to investigate the potential of educational technology (e.g., television, video, computers). Here are some readings along these lines:

Ball, J., and Jamison, D. "Computer-Assisted Instruction for Dispersed Populations: Systems Cost Models." *Instructional Science 1* (1972/1973): 469–501.

Kopstein, F., and Seidel, R. J. "Computer Administered Instruction versus Traditionally Administered Instruction: Economics." *AVCR* 16 (Summer 1968): 147–175.

Kielt, J. P., and Spitzer, D. R. "Costing Educational Technology: Some Promising Approaches." *Educational Technology* (March 1975): 42–45.

Kearsley, G. P. "The Cost of CAI: A Matter of Assumptions." *AEDS Journal* (Summer 1977): 100–112.

Mayo, J. K., et al. "The Mexican Telesecundaria: A Cost-Effectiveness Analysis." *Instructional Science* 1 (1975): 193–236.

Orlansky, J., and String, J. "Cost-Effectiveness of Computer-Based Instruction in Military Training." Institute for Defense Analysis P-1375, Arlington, Va., April 1979 (NTIS: AD073400).

Roscoe, S. N. "Transfer and Cost Effectiveness of Ground-Based Flight Trainers." In S. Roscoe, *Aviation Psychology*. Ames: Iowa State Press, 1980.

Seidel, R. J. "It's 1980: Do Your Know Where Your Computer Is?" *Phi Delta Kappan* (March 1980): 481–485.

Seidel, R. J., and Wagner, H. "A Cost-Effectiveness Specification." In H. O'Neil, ed. *Procedures for Instructional Systems Development*. New York: Academic Press, 1979.

Van der Drift, K. D. J. M. "Cost Effectiveness of Audiovisual Media in Higher Education." *Instructional Science* 9 (1980): 355–364.

Wells, S. "Cost Analysis of Televised Instruction for Continuing Professional Education." *Instructional Science* 6 (1977): 259–282.

Appendix

Answers to the Problems

Chapter Three: Resource Requirements Model

The costs of the existing regional training approach are shown in Figure A–1. The costs of the proposed decentralized approach are shown in Figure A–2. According to this analysis the centralized approach would save $11,000 annually ($848,000–$837,000). While this is probably not the substantial savings the director of the agency was hoping for, it seems likely that it would result in a significant improvement in training effectiveness due to the availability of new and better equipment. Of course, this would have to be shown in an evaluation study. Note: There are many more costs that would have to be taken into account if this was a real problem, such as the salvage value of the equipment at the regional centers, the relocation expenses of the instructors, etc.

	Personnel	Facilities	Equipment	Materials	
Analysis					
Design					
Development					
Implementation	4 x $30,000 4 x 200 x $250 4 x 200 x $500	4 x $12,000	4 x $20,000		
Evaluation					$812,000
	$720,000	$48,000	$80,000		$848,000

Figure A-1 Resource Requirements Matrix

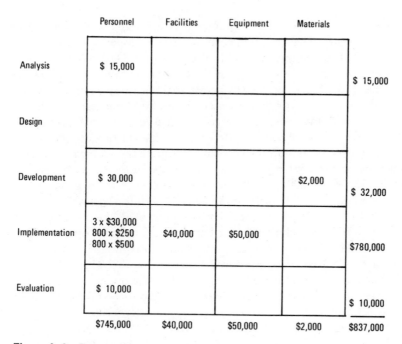

	Personnel	Facilities	Equipment	Materials	
Analysis	$ 15,000				$ 15,000
Design					
Development	$ 30,000			$2,000	$ 32,000
Implementation	3 x $30,000 800 x $250 800 x $500	$40,000	$50,000		$780,000
Evaluation	$ 10,000				$ 10,000
	$745,000	$40,000	$50,000	$2,000	$837,000

Figure A-2 Resource Requirements Matrix

Chapter Four: Life Cycle Cost Models

In this example we are comparing the costs of the new system against the potential savings of one less day of training ($200 per manager). The total amount that could be saved in a year is $200 × 800 managers = $160,000. Our life cycle costs for the new self-study approach are:

Total Life
Cycle Costs = R&D + Startup + Transition + Steady State
(5 years)   Costs   Costs   Costs   Costs

The R&D costs were $32,000 for the pilot study. The startup costs are $40,000 for facility conversion and $60,000 for equipment. Amortized over three years, the annual equipment cost is $20,000 for each of the first three years. The transition costs are the development costs, which is either $180,000 for the six-month alternative or $120,000 for the one-year alternative, and the salary of the temporary instructor, which will be either $18,000 for six months or $36,000 for a year. The steady state costs include instructor salaries, operating and maintenance costs, etc. The operating and maintenance cost of the equipment ($6,000) is the only steady state cost that is different from the existing approach.

Before we can sum up the costs and compute the savings, we need to select the best transition period. The total cost of a six-month transition is $180,000 + $18,000 = $198,000; the total cost of the one-year transition is $120,000 + $36,000 = $156,000. The difference is $198,000 − $156,000 = $42,000. The annual cost savings of the new approach (which cannot be achieved until the program is fully operational) is $160,000. Thus, if the program is implemented six months earlier, a savings of $80,000 could be produced. This means that although the six-month transition will cost $42,000 more than the one-year transition, it can save $80,000. The cost-effective decision would be to choose the six-month transition.

We can now calculate the life cycle costs:

Total Life
Cycle Costs = $32,000 + ($40,000 + $60,000) + $198,000
(5 years)   3 years   6 mos.
          + (5 × $6,000) = $360,000

From this calculation, we can see that the total life cycle savings for five years are:

Total Life
Cycle Cost = (5 × $160,000) − $360,000 = $440,000
Savings
(5 years)

The break-even point would be 2.3 years, i.e., by the end of the third year, the new self-study approach would be generating a cost savings. The cost savings for the steady state period (years 4 and 5) would be $160,000 − $6,000 = $152,000 each year.

Chapter Five: Benefits Analysis Models

The derived weights for the model are shown in Figure A–3. As far as the difference between videotape and videodisc on accident rates is concerned, the benefits analysis suggests that the use of videodisc could result in a potential improvement of 8 percent (.12 versus .04) over videotape. Looking at the magnitude of the differences for the various outcomes, it appears that learning strategies (.7 versus .04) and amount of practice (.7 versus .2) show the greatest differences between videotape and videodisc.

To determine which attribute results in the greatest difference between videotape and videodisc, we need to do a sensitivity analysis. This means we zero out each of the four attributes one at a time and see what the values of the derived outcomes are. If you do the sensitivity analysis, you will find that presentation capabilities have the greatest effect.

Chapter Six: Productivity Models

The estimated development costs for each of the three alternative media mixes are:

$$Alternative\ 1 = 10(10)^{1.1} + 60(10)^{1.2} + 100(10)^{1.5}$$
$$= \$10 \times (1100 + 7200 + 15000)$$
$$= \$233,000$$

$$Alternative\ 2 = 10(15)^{1.1} + 60(10)^{1.2} + 100(5)^{1.5}$$
$$= \$10 \times (4400 + 7200 + 3750)$$
$$= \$134,250$$

$$Alternative\ 3 = 10(20)^{1.1} + 60(5)^{1.2} + 100(5)^{1.5}$$
$$= \$10 \times (4400 + 1800 + 3750)$$
$$= \$99,500$$

Alternative 3 is the least expensive media mix. If the total development costs must be reduced by 20 percent, the media mix would be fifteen hours of workbook, four hours of slide/tape, and four hours of CBI.

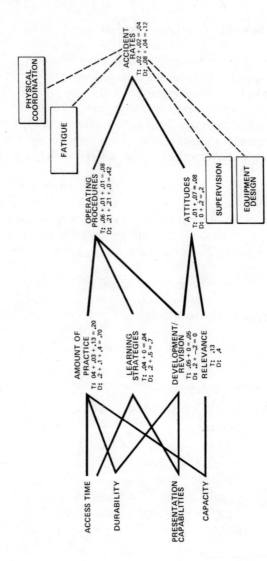

Figure A-3 Causal Model with Derived Weights

(Note that usually different media involve different types of development staff and facilities and, hence, each media would be multiplied by different unit costs rather than a single rate.)

Chapter Nine: Case Study

There are four possible outcomes of the meeting and, hence, of the case study:

1. The committee is convinced by your thorough presentation that the OATS training program is essential and that they should fund the self-study multimedia approach for subsequent OATS training. They give the go-ahead to proceed with your plans.

2. The committee is convinced by your thorough presentation that the OATS training program is essential and that they should fund the self-study multimedia approach for subsequent OATS training. However, the company simply does not have the money to fund OATS training at the level you need. They ask you to come up with a less costly approach, accepting the fact that this will result in a lower level of OATS utilizaton and proficiency.

3. The committee is convinced by your presentation that the OATS training program is essential, but they are not completely convinced that the self-study approach is the best approach to future training. A number of members raise concerns about whether self-study training will work for everyone and whether the video component (which requires the purchase of new equipment) is really essential. The committee asks you to develop a plan that involves a combination of both instructor-based and self-study training so they can be compared on a better basis.

4. The committee is not completely convinced by your presentation that the OATS training program is essential or that the self-study multimedia approach is the best plan for subsequent OATS training. In fact, some of the committee members are not sure OATS is such a good idea anymore. You realize that the success of OATS has begun

to change the power structure of the organization and some committee members are very threatened by their loss of control. You decide to retreat for the moment and ask for more time to study other training alternatives. Before the next meeting, you will have to make sure that general resistance to OATS (and, hence, OATS training) is eliminated. This means changing the attitudes of each opponent through one-on-one discussions.

Chapter Twelve: Summing Up

Of course, this scenario does not have anything to do with cost/benefits analysis in particular. However, it does make an important point. Even though you may have conducted an outstanding cost/benefits analysis that is convincing beyond the shadow of a doubt, there are always good reasons why you still may not succeed. This example illustrates a common one: more demands for a fixed budget than can be satisfied.

So what could you do in this situation? Clearly, the need for more cars and salary increases is just as important and justified as the need for your training program. One possible suggestion is that the available money is split three ways, allowing each need to be addressed. Unfortunately, this democratic solution often does not work—the resulting amount may be insufficient to have any real effect. A better suggestion is to find a solution that allows the synthesis of all three problems. Could the community relations program be handled by senior officers (for higher pay) and without the use of squad cars? It is unlikely, but worth a look. Cost/benefits analysis has been known to lead to strange bedfellows on many occasions!

Coda: Training problems are often complex and cost/benefits analysis is hardly a substitute for common sense, ingenuity, and good insight.

Index

Index